IN THE
WAITING

*Encouraging Words
for Difficult Times*

TIM HAWS

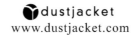

www.dustjacket.com

DEDICATION

This book is dedicated to my family:
Lisa, Jackson, Grayson, and Hudson.

Thanks for listening time and again to all my stories.
You are greatly loved!

CONTENTS

ACKNOWLEDGMENTS

This book would not have been possible without the help of Adam Toler at Dust Jacket Publishing. The Toler family continues to greatly impact the Haws family and the kingdom of God. Jonathan Wright, your help and insight in editing and organizing this book were amazing. Bob and Edith Ely, your encouragement and help getting this whole thing started have been incredible. Finally, I must brag on the one God has used to make me a better person: my wife, Lisa. You are a perfect example of God blessing me beyond what I could ever hope or imagine.

FOREWORD

It looked like a routine tackle. Then it looked like a routine injury. I started out toward the field with Kyle, our athletic trainer, to see what Hudson had injured.

Little did I know that I was encountering a situation that would change the lives of so many people forever. Walking out onto the field, I felt the frustration of looking at another player lying on the turf with an injury. At that point I was still worried about the game, the score, the playoff standings. Injuries are part of football, of course, so much so that coaches and players can easily become calloused to them. Not that we don't have some sympathy for an injured player, but the question a coach gets to quickly is "How long will he be out?" A life-threatening or life-changing injury is so rare that our minds rarely consider it. My initial thought was that Hudson had gotten his "bell rung" and that he was going to be out the rest of this game and more than likely the next week since generally a concussion would take at least seven to ten days to heal.

As I got closer, however, I noticed that he was lying face down in an awkward position and obviously had not moved. I thought, "Did he get knocked unconscious? If so, he'll probably be out at least two weeks or more. Our defense is really going to be in trouble!"

As I knelt down beside Hudson, I realized that he was conscious, so I asked him, "What's wrong?"

"I can't move!" he replied.

That was not the first time I had heard this statement from a player but it still sent a chill through me, as it always does. Several times in my career I had heard this when a player had a mild neck or shoulder injury. All those times their sensation and movement had returned within a few minutes. I've even seen a few players carted off the field on a stretcher and taken to the emergency room by ambulance only to be released shortly afterward with a sore neck but otherwise unharmed.

Kyle quickly began to access the injury. I watched him squeeze Hudson's leg and ask if he could feel it.

"No," Hudson replied.

Then he squeezed Hudson's arm and asked if he could feel it.

"Yes," Hudson said.

I felt a sense of relief that maybe this would be like those other instances and his feeling was coming back. But it was not—he still could not feel his lower body. I took his hand and squeezed it. I could feel him weakly attempt to squeeze back. The scene on the field in Blanchard, Oklahoma, was growing more concerning for onlookers. Hudson's father, Tim, had just joined us on the field as the local paramedics were stepping in and Kyle had begun to immobilize Hudson's head by holding it securely with both hands. The paramedic continued pinching different areas of Hudson's lower body. I noticed that each pinch grew increasingly harder and each time Hudson answered no to the repeated question "Can you feel this?"

The fear and urgency of the situation began to amplify. A decision was made to have Hudson flown from Blanchard by helicopter to a hospital in nearby Oklahoma City. I looked at our sideline and saw our players huddled together in prayer. I will never forget the silence of the entire stadium.

Notes and Thoughts

- I think of the days, weeks, and years that followed this terrible night. Most people will look at Hudson's injury and use expressions like *sad, tragedy, terrible, awful, life-changing* to describe it. All these descriptions are accurate, of course, but there's also another side, where *love* and *faith* prevailed. Hudson and his family could have easily cursed God or asked, "Why us?" becoming bitter and angry. But they chose to love harder and trust God even more.

- Love is an action, not just a feeling, and I had never before seen love in action more powerfully than in this situation. I saw love for a son, a brother, a friend, a family, and a community.

- Seeing a player writhing in pain is now somewhat a relief— because if he is moving and hurting, he is not paralyzed.

- How did God bring good out of a tragic situation? Hudson and his family's faith, of course. Tim's emotions, wisdom, and faith poured out by words and stories were shared, along with the power of friendship.

- Hudson will end up helping, encouraging, and inspiring more people than would have been possible had this tragedy not befallen him.

Unconditional love
Unconditional faith
Unconditional commitment

—Reagan Roof
Former dean of students and head football coach
Bethany (Okla.) High School
Currently athletic director and head football coach
Weatherford (Okla.) High School

INTRODUCTION

Life keeps throwing me curve balls—
and I don't even own a bat. At least my
dodging skills are improving!
—Jayleigh Cape

If you're reading this book, chances are that life has thrown you a curve ball or two. Some of you have just recently joined the ranks of those who are going through hard times. Others have been walking through the valley for a while. My family has faced its share of hard times over the years, but nothing compared to the events of October 23, 2015, when our youngest son, Hudson, suffered a spinal cord injury while participating in a high school football game in Blanchard, Oklahoma. The fracture of a couple of cervical vertebrae instantly and radically changed his life and the story of our family.

My wife, Lisa, and I met in junior high while attending church camp. After that first meeting, it only took me another six years to ask her out on a date. Three years later we were married. While I finished up my undergraduate degree, Lisa was completing law school. I soon began my career as a public school teacher and coach while Lisa began her law career. We welcomed our first son, Jackson, into the world in 1991, followed by his brother Grayson in 1994. Four years later, Hudson joined the ranks as the third installment of my three sons.

We decided to put Lisa's career on hold after Jackson was born so she could stay home with the Haws boys. Lisa poured herself into their lives and did an awesome job of keeping our home operating like a well-oiled machine. All three of our boys shared the same bedroom for nearly a decade. Living in such tight quarters developed a close relationship between them despite seven years from the birth of Jackson and Hudson.

Our boys were active in sports from an early age. We have spent our share of time at the ballpark or in a gym throughout central Oklahoma. We have made many friends and developed countless memories during those years. It was in Hudson's senior year of high school with just a handful of games left when he was hurt. Hudson's injury has impacted each of us in a profound way.

When we entered what the Bible refers to as "the valley of the shadow of death," I discovered that this valley was crowded with folks dealing with the loss of loved ones, unexpected medical diagnoses, addictions, lack of resources and security—the list goes on and on. Maybe you are a recent visitor here. There are a several things I have learned through my journey in this valley. It can be a scary place. Most everyone is weary.

About the time you think it can't get any darker, it does. You somehow get used to hanging out at the end of your rope.

Yet through all the dark, scary times, I have also experienced the power of prayer and an encouraging word. I've learned that God loves to hang out in places I never imagined. He also loves to send special agents to minister to those in need. They show up at just the right time with just the right words.

During Hudson's three-month rehab at Craig Hospital in Denver, I would post updates for family and friends. These were my thoughts and feelings as a dad whose kid was experiencing tragedy. I also began journaling what God was laying on my heart. It wasn't long before people began to encourage me to put a book together. I have resisted for years for a number of reasons. One is the lack of confidence in my abilities. You may concur with that assessment after you read a few pages. The biggest reason is Hudson. My son is reserved and not a seeker of the spotlight. He is tough, does not complain, and amazes me every day. I didn't want to cause him any anxiety. Hudson has given me the green light to move forward—which leads me to the purpose of this book: to speak encouragement and words of hope into your situation.

My next challenge was to sort through the hundreds of stories I have written and combine them so they would have some sort of flow. This proved to be quite the challenge. Many of my stories were written during Hudson's first three months in the hospital. Others were written during subsequent hospital stays due to infection or as we moved day to day through life.

As a reader you will bounce around to various stops along our journey. This roller coaster of events reflects the life of a family dealing with a chronic injury or disease.

These stories are a collection of events that have shaped my life and are intertwined in my view of God. Most were brought back to memory as I sought answers and guidance through prayer and my reading of the Bible. This combination of memories and scripture has continued to point me to my source of hope—Jesus. My prayer is that this book will shine a light in your dark place, to remind you that we have a Savior who can reverse the impossible, transform ugly and tragic circumstances into more than we could ever imagine or hope.

Our God is still in the miracle business. While we are still in the waiting, it's encouraging to know that we are not alone. So we hang in there—one day at a time. I hope you will too.

1

At the Feet of Jesus

The news spread through the region like wildfire: Jesus of Nazareth was on His way. The rumor mill was working overtime and the stories were too good to be true: Jesus can change the impossible; broken bodies are made whole; crushed spirits are renewed; relationships are mended; forgiveness is found.

The streets began filling as family members hauled their loved ones toward the hill on the edge of town. There were tons of them. The blind were being led by the hand, the paralyzed hauled on makeshift mats. Young people, clearly under the influence of something, were being guided by brokenhearted parents. Men, women, and children stumbled down the street on the edge of death as diseases ate away at their bodies. The hint of a chance that this Jesus could change their impossible to possible was all they needed.

A cry rose above the sounds of the procession. His attendance was validated as people began to call out the name of

Jesus. Then they saw Him. Jesus had moved up the hill and sat down on a large rock, ready to receive visitors. The hope in the crowd was electric. *Hope.* Many in the crowd had forgotten what it felt like to genuinely hope. They had hung on for years with eager expectation of something to change, but the days had taken their toll.

Some in the crowd voiced skepticism. Most just tried to bury their doubts deep within their hearts. Maybe it was just a protection mechanism honed by past disappointments. Everyone knew the stories of old. Rabbis recited from memory how God had moved over and over in miraculous ways to rescue His people from bondage. Even small children could provide the details of David's defeat of Goliath. The excitement of those victories had paled over time, now replaced with questions. Was God still with them? Did He care? Does God hear our prayers? Do they make a difference?

There were still some who believed, and their encouragement and examples were contagious. Their faithful prayers and acts of kindness gave many the strength to make it one more day. Regardless of where they stood before, today they had one thing in common: Jesus was coming to their region, and the chance that things could change moved them into action.

All eyes were on the first groups of family members as they approached Jesus, loved ones in tow. They more or less threw them down at Jesus' feet to see what He would do with them. Thousands held their collective breath, faces fixed on the scene. Jesus looked at the people laid at His feet and then at the crowd.

What they didn't realize was that He knew them all by name. They were standing on dirt He had created, kneeling on grass He had spoken into being. Jesus also saw the condition of their hearts. He saw the doubt, pain, questions, and sin. I wonder if He had to hide a smile as His plan was coming together. Those He had called to Him this day were here and He was ready to reveal His true character. He healed them.

When the people saw the mutes speaking, the maimed healthy, the quadriplegics walking, the blind looking around, they were astonished. Things got crazy for the next several minutes as people pushed forward in search of healing. They had no idea that this spring of living water was endless. Some of Jesus' disciples got things under control and soon something resembling a line slowly filtered toward a knot of people. You couldn't see Jesus anymore; His location was marked by the shouts of praise, rejoicing, cries of freedom. The news made it back home and more people came. Some of those who were healed ran back to town to get a buddy who needed help. Soon lines of people could be seen flowing to Jesus from all directions.

Matthew 15 tells us that this went on for three days. The wonderful news is that this same Jesus is here with us today, at this very moment—the same Jesus who can transform the impossible to the possible, the same Jesus who still receives the broken. Many of you have brought someone you know and love to the feet of Jesus. Like the people near that lake in Galilee, we sometimes wonder what chance there is for healing. I love the words of Jesus: "Every chance in the world if you trust God to do it" (Matthew 19:26 MSG).

The people were amazed when they saw the mute speaking, the crippled made well, the lame walking and the blind seeing. And they praised the God of Israel (Matthew 15:31).

✝✝

—+— 2 —+—

Can You Hear Me Now?

I was not born with exceptional athletic ability. I don't have incredible strength, nor do I tower above others. I have worn glasses since early elementary school and have documented the vision challenges I face. However, I was gifted with one thing: the ability to hear. This probably comes as a shock to all the people who warned me in my teenage years to turn down my stereo. Many of the teachers I have worked with will testify to the fact that my ears work. They will also testify that I still like to play my music loudly! The only two people I know who might argue about the accuracy of my hearing would be my wife and my mom.

My ability to pick up sound has served me well, especially since I work with young people. I used to be able to sleep through the night—nothing could wake me up. Then we had kids. If Jackson even rolled over I sprang to attention. I haven't slept through the night since December 19, 1991.

I've done some reading on hearing. Audiologists say that if you score from -10 dB to 25 dB on a hearing test, you are normal. But there are big differences within the normal range. For instance, a person at -10 dB hears a thousand times better than someone who hears at 20 dB. This hearing scale is determined by a ratio between a measured level of sound and a set standard. That standard happens to be 10 to the minus 12 watts per square meter in case you are interested. This standard is set at the volume of the faintest sound the average person with "perfect" hearing can just barely hear.

That's just here on earth. If you go out to space, you would hear nothing. All those X-Wing and Tie Fighter battles were rigged by the movies. Space is a vacuum. Sound needs air to work. Since there is no air in space, the big explosion of the Death Star was just a silent light show. What amazes me even more is the fact that there are people who have figured all this stuff out.

I've spent a lot of time listening intently from a tree stand. I use my ears even more than my eyes when trying to detect a whitetail deer. I listen for any sound that may indicate the presence of Mr. Big. It's amazing what we can hear when we slow down and listen. I mean *really* listen—for more than ten seconds.

I've been practicing listening a lot lately, listening intently, hoping to hear the voice of Jesus reassure me. I was watching a television show recently and noticed a lady holding a necklace with a cross on it. I got the message without a word being spoken.

God knows what it feels like when someone you love is hurting. He heard His Son's words before they even rolled off His tongue. As Jesus hung on the cross, He began quoting Psalm 22. I can relate to that song. Sometimes I feel as if God is a million miles away and can't hear my cries. Trouble is near and there seems to be no one to help—basically the same words Jesus spoke on the day when He allowed them to nail Him to a cross for our sins. God heard every word.

Then I turn the page and see Psalm 23. The Lord is my Shepherd—I am not alone. He refreshes my soul, He pours Himself into me. He guides me, even when it's so dark I cannot see where He has taken me. He anoints me with His presence. He has heard my cries.

God hears us better than -10 dB, for He knows our needs and words before they roll off our tongues. God can hear our cries even in outer space.

Over the last couple of months I have been listening intently. I continually talk with God about Hudson. The only audible voice I have heard is my own. That's the case not simply these last several months. I have never heard the audible voice of God. Just because I haven't heard God audibly doesn't mean He isn't speaking.

As I looked out the window at Craig Hospital I saw the beautiful Rocky Mountains. They spoke to me. The tree across the street, an MRI of a spinal cord, a goose, all of God's creation speaks to me. The message is clear: "Look what I can do. My power and ability are beyond your comprehension."

God chooses to let His creation speak for itself—no big announcements saying, "Hey! Did you see that sunset I painted this evening?" It's the proverbial picture painting a thousand words. Like a cross and an empty tomb, a clear pathology report, and an empty wheelchair—I hear Him loud and clear. He loves us.

Come and hear, all you who fear God;
let me tell you what he has done for me. I cried out to
him with my mouth; his praise was on my tongue. If I
had cherished sin in my heart, the Lord would not have
listened; but God has surely listened and has heard my
prayer. Praise be to God, who has not rejected my
prayer or withheld his love from me!
(Psalm 66:16–20).

3

In the Magic

We are a Disney family. We took our first trip to Disneyland in 2004. To tell you the truth, I wasn't pumped about going to a theme park. I'm more of an amusement park guy. I just couldn't get fired up over the images of spinning teacups and flying elephants.

Lisa and I had saved our money for this family vacation and we were going to make the most of it for the boys. We drove to California with a pit stop in Flagstaff, Arizona. We showed up to the gates an hour before the park officially opened—obviously still operating on Oklahoma time. I immediately sensed that something was different about this place. Everything was immaculate. The flower beds were perfect. The lines were well organized. The people who worked there were called "cast members." The music drifting over the air was cheerful and friendly.

By the time the train came rolling down the track, I was already hooked. We had somehow walked through some portal into a land that invited you to have a good morning. Every song and dance informed you that you were going to have a magical time. They invited you to use your imagination and to make some memories. Everyone had a smile on his or her face—except maybe that four-year-old whose brother just broke his Mickey ears, or maybe the gentleman who didn't understand why last year's fast pass was not going to work this year.

We spent the next several days "in the magic," hopping back and forth between Disneyland and its sister theme park, California Adventure. I remember Hudson being just tall enough to ride most of the rides. We had to teach him "the stretch" since he was right on the edge of ride disqualification. There's nothing worse than having to take the walk of shame back through the crowd due to the fact that you're not tall enough to ride. As soon as we spied the cast member approaching with the measuring rod, we would call out our secret code word, *rutabaga*, and Hudson would break into his stretch mode. We were relieved every time they said, "You're good to go." And go we did!

Hudson's favorite ride was Space Mountain. I think we rode most every ride numerous times. I say "most" because we got stuck in the middle of the "It's a Small World" ride for about a half hour. Unfortunately, the car wouldn't move but the music kept right on playing—the same theme song over and over again. By the time we got off I felt as if I had been through some sort of newfangled torture scheme. I shudder to this day every time I walk by that ride entrance and hear the music in the background.

We have made several return trips to Disneyland and also to the Magic Kingdom at Disney World in Florida. My favorite activity of all at these parks is people-watching. I love finding a vacant rocking chair in Frontierland and simply watching the people walk by as banjos and steel guitars play in the background. I get a kick out of watching kids get mesmerized by a character, ride, or event that they may have watched in a movie or read about. It's one thing to have seen the *Pirates of the Caribbean* movie, but it's another to actually float down a river through the mist and trees of the ride, listening to Captain Jack Sparrow sing, "Yo ho, yo ho, a pirate's life for me!"

Disney reminds me a lot of the kingdom of God. When you enter it, you feel something different. It is that "place" your soul has been looking to find. It's not without its challenges and occasional tears. The big difference is that God's kingdom does not have a measuring rod. If you choose to come, He doesn't require you to stretch to meet a certain height or submit to a bag check. He just beckons, "Good morning," to all who want to enter. Once you enter, you discover He doesn't people-watch; rather, He people-interacts. He's on the ride with us— the fun and relaxing rides as well as the scary and heart-pounding ones. And what's really awesome is that we don't have to use our imaginations—it's real.

The transformation that God works in us has a theme, too, and it's love. He loves us. Oh, how He loves us! I long for our next trip to Disney as a family. It serves as a huge reminder to me of all the kingdom of God holds for us. At this point I could probably even be talked into getting on "It's a Small World" again. Now *that's* scary!

> *The Lord has established his throne in heaven,*
> *and his kingdom rules over all*
> (Psalm 103:19).

And When You Pray

I'm terrible at golf. I wish I weren't, but I am. Those guys on television make it look so easy. What makes golf really frustrating is that every once in a great while I will actually hit a successful golf shot—but all that does is give me delusions of grandeur. I play only a few times a year, and then usually part of a team of four. My main job is to make the other members of my group feel better about their game. All I have to say is that you had better be paying attention when I'm swinging away—there's no telling where that ball is going to end up!

Golf is a game that requires you to put in your practice time—in my case, a great deal of time. I believe this is also true if one wants to have an effective prayer life. My prayer life has changed a lot since my son was injured. I wish I could say it had not changed; I wish I had always prayed like this. But that wouldn't be the truth. I am a firm believer that God is always looking for opportunities to get our attention. Whether through prayer, His creation, His written Word, preachers, teachers, or music, God is constantly speaking to us. I have well received the messages He sends me through His creation. Those are crystal clear. I have also heard my fair share of sermons and have been blessed by many of them. Over the last month I have listened to worship songs that I feel were written exclusively for our current situation.

When I look at the example Jesus set, I feel I have missed the mark when it comes to prayer and God's Word. Throughout Scripture we hear Jesus quoting God's written Word to us. That's right: quoting, not reading from a scroll—scripture put to memory, written on His heart. I don't think Jesus actually had to do that because He *is* the Word. He is God's Word become flesh. So why all the quoting and memorization? As an example for us.

We also read throughout the gospels about Jesus praying, sometimes short prayers and sometimes all night. He prayed prayers of thanksgiving and prayers of pain and suffering. He prayed in public and He prayed by Himself. If anything is crystal clear to me, it is that my Bible reading and prayer life got watered down over time. My pastor, Rick Harvey, has said some things that have really resonated with me recently. He has reminded us that we need to frequently visit and revisit God's Word to remind us of who He is and the promises He has made. If history shows nothing else, it screams that we have poor memories and need constant reminders. We need ingrained within ourselves those things that are vital. Another thing Pastor Harvey recently asked was "Does the devil say, 'Oh, no—he's awake!' when you roll out of bed?"

It's my desire for the rest of my life to communicate with God as effectively as my biblical heroes. I believe that what we declare as miracles that happened in biblical times can, should, and do happen today. I want to be an active part of all God sends my way. I ask you to join me in a prayer revolution. The change has to begin within each of us, and I strongly believe that any change must be centered on Jesus. He is the source of all transformation because it is Jesus we seek to mirror.

Some of you have already figured all of this out. You are way down the road from where I am. I just want you to know that I'm on my way!

Is anyone among you in trouble? Let them pray.
Is anyone happy? Let them sing songs of praise. Is anyone
among you sick? Let them call the elders of the church to
pray over them and anoint them with oil in the name of the
Lord. And the prayer offered in faith will make the sick person
well; the Lord will raise them up. If they have sinned, they
will be forgiven. Therefore confess your sins to each other
and pray for each other so that you may be healed. The prayer
of a righteous person is powerful and effective
(James 5:13–16).

5

Loaded for Bear

When I was ten years old and visiting an aunt and uncle's house, my cousin and I decided to go fishing. A pond across the road was calling our names and enticing us with visions of landing a lunker. We grabbed our fishing gear, along with a thermos of red Kool-Aid, and off we went.

As we made our way across the pasture we heard a commotion off to our right. Three or four men were running toward us, yelling and screaming. While we just stood there trying to figure out what was going on, we spotted another object moving in our direction. At first we thought our eyes were playing tricks on us but soon realized: a huge bear was hightailing it right for us. It had chains attached to its neck that were bouncing and clanking as it ran. I froze, looked at my cousin, and then we both took off running as fast as we could in the opposite direction.

There were some homes under construction to the south of us. We raced toward them and the little protection the framed structures appeared to offer. When we reached the first construction site, we jumped around the corner of a nearly completed home. I was breathing heavily with my head on a swivel, making sure Smokey wasn't about to surprise-attack us.

All of a sudden my cousin started screaming and asking me if I was okay. I was like, "Yes, but if you keep screaming I may *not* be!" He grabbed me and spun me around as if looking for something. I told him to stop and asked what in the world he was doing. I then noticed my pants and shirt were stained red. While running I had dropped my fishing pole but had held on to the thermos of Kool-Aid. The lid wasn't on tightly, and the red fluid had gotten all over my shirt and shorts. My cousin thought I was bleeding.

We waited several anxious minutes before we made a dash for my aunt and uncle's house. When we showed up and told our story, no one believed us. They thought we were seeing things. I found out later that the Clyde Brothers Circus wintered their animals in the area. I've always been thankful that it wasn't an escaped *cheetah* chasing us that day!

Recently I was going through some of our old baseball gear and found a book by Mark Batterson titled *In a Pit with a Lion on a Snowy Day*. It was a gift from my good friend Tal and is about one of David's mighty warriors from 2 Samuel 23. I read about Benaiah, a guy from Kabzeel, who went down into a pit and killed a lion on a snowy day. Now I don't know what they feed guys from Kabzeel, but I need some of whatever they're having for dinner.

To intentionally go into a dark, small, enclosed pit containing a lion takes some bravery. Not ordinary bravery—*extraordinary* bravery. I don't think the odds were in Benaiah's favor that day. Most of us would have given the nod to an animal designed to kill and eat.

It wasn't the only time the odds were against Benaiah. He also had to battle another country's two mightiest warriors. Two on one—not good odds. Benaiah fought a huge Egyptian who was armed with a spear. Benaiah had only a club. He ended up defeating the Egyptian with the guy's own spear. Benaiah later got a job as King David's bodyguard. I think David loved hiring lion killers.

Earlier this week a doctor made some comments to me about Hudson and statistical odds. He didn't spell them out specifically but used the phrase "The odds are not in your favor." I wonder how many people thought the same thing about Benaiah. I agree with Mark Batterson when he writes,

> There is a pattern that I see repeated throughout Scripture: Sometimes God won't intervene until something is humanly impossible. And He usually does it just in the nick of time. I think that pattern reveals one dimension of God's personality: God loves impossible odds. . . . God sometimes invites us to defy impossible odds. Maybe it is one way He can show us His omnipotence. Maybe God allows the odds to be stacked against us so He can reveal more of His glory.

Mr. Batterson in his book *ID: The True You* reminds us of the story of Gideon in Judges 6. God has an army of 32,000 men and they are vastly outnumbered by the Midianites. Judges 6:5 says it was "impossible to count" them. So the odds are already at least 100:1. Then the Lord says, "You have too many men for me to deliver Midian into their hands." If I'm Gideon I'm thinking God misspoke. "You said 'too many' but what you really meant to say was 'too few.'"

The Lord says, "You heard me right. You've got too many men." And He tells Gideon to get rid of anyone who is afraid. Gideon loses two-thirds of his army—22,000 out of 32,000 go home! He's left with ten thousand and the odds are up to 10,000:1.

Then the Lord says in verse 4, "There are still too many men." So God devises a test. Gideon's army goes to get a drink of water and God tells him to get rid of the men who drink like a dog and another 9,700 are eliminated. Gideon is left with an "army" of 300 men. And the odds go up to 1,000,000:1.

And it gets better!

God tells Gideon to attack the Midianites with trumpets and jars! You've got to be kidding me! What kind of battle is that? And here's the kicker: Israel wins!

Why does God do it that way? Judges 7:2 tells us why. God defeats the Midianites with 300 Israelites instead of 32,000 Israelites so that "Israel may not boast against me that her own strength has saved her."

I have a bear of another kind chasing me these days. It produces the same fear as the one forty years ago. This bear is loaded with doubt and wants to remind me all the time how the odds are stacked against us. The bear arrogantly invites me to crawl down into the pit and take him on. Then I feel a hand on my shoulder. It is God's mighty Warrior. He is also a lover of impossible odds. He tells me that I don't have to do this one alone.

Are the odds not in *your* favor either? Down in a pit? Got something that seems impossible? Facing 1,000,000:1 odds? Come join us! We're right where God wants us to be. We're trusting Him, poised on the edge of our seats waiting to see His glory.

Then Jesus said, "Did I not tell you that if you believe,
you will see the glory of God?"
(John 11:40).

Clean-up on Aisle 7

I remember one Christmas when my mom took us to the local TG&Y variety store to do our Christmas shopping. We made our mom stay in the car, which was parked just outside the exit, so she wouldn't see what we were getting her for Christmas. I grabbed my basket and weaved my way up and down the aisles looking for just the right gift. I would try to elude my brother and sister because I didn't want them to see what I was getting them either.

As I glided amongst the displays, my mind was on overload. Should I get this or that? Will I have enough money to pay for all of this? Did my sister see her gift? As I rounded a corner, I misjudged the swing of my basket and struck a one-foot-tall ceramic Santa and knocked it over. The problem was that it just happened to be on the bottom row of a pyramid of Santas that were stacked ten feet tall. It turned into one of those slow-motion moments you sometimes have in life. The slight totter of the pivotal Santa turned into an avalanche of red, white, and black spilling all around me. I think the roar of breaking glass broke the sound barrier.

When the dust had settled, I was surrounded by shattered Santas. My first instinct was to run but I didn't have an escape route. Then I look around to see every person in the store sticking their head around a corner to see what had blown up. My sister came walking toward me with her usual "You're in trouble" look. I knew that look well because she would send it my way every Sunday right before I got jerked out of the service for an "attitude adjustment." Fear began setting in.

My sister started wading through the arms, legs, and torsos and asked me if I was okay. That's it! My mind began to race. Maybe I am seriously injured and have to go to the hospital and everyone will forget what I had just done! I began searching for signs of injury. As I scanned my clothes, desperately looking for blood, I noticed someone who appeared to be a store manager heading my way. If I could have willed blood to pour from every orifice of my body, I would have.

All I could do is stand there. In the eyes of a child the store manager looked to be about six feet eight inches tall and an easy two hundred seventy-five pounds. He crunched his way through the glass, picked me up, and carried me out of the disaster area. After setting me down, he asked if I was okay. I whispered that I was and began to pull my money out of my pocket. Even with my primary math skills I knew that I didn't have enough money to pay for what I had just done. The debt I owed was beyond my imagination.

My dad always used to joke that if we didn't have enough money to pay for a meal, we would have to go wash dishes. The thought crossed my mind that I would be washing dishes at TG&Y for the rest of my life. By this time the tears were flowing and I could hardly speak. I thrust my wad of money and change toward the manager. I will never forget what he said to me: "Young man, you put that money back in your pocket. I know you didn't mean to knock that over, and besides, we probably had them stacked too high anyway. I'm just glad you're okay." I just stared at him in disbelief. I didn't know what to say. He took me over and rang up the stuff I had in my basket and checked me out.

I don't know if that manager was a Christian, but he taught me a lesson of the true meaning of Christmas that I have never forgotten. I owed a debt I could not pay. I was guilty and needed a redeemer.

And there were shepherds [kids] *living out in the fields nearby* [shopping at TG&Y], *keeping watch over their flocks at night* [standing in the middle of some broken Santas]. *An angel of the Lord appeared to them* [dressed as a manager], *and the glory of the Lord shone around them, and they were terrified. But the angel said to them, "Do not be afraid. I bring you good news that will cause great joy for all the people. Today in the town of David a Savior has been born to you; He is the Messiah, the Lord.*

This will be a sign to you: You will find a baby wrapped in cloths and lying in a manger." Suddenly a great company of the heavenly host appeared with the angel, praising God and saying, "Glory to God in the highest heaven, and on earth peace to those on whom his favor rests" (Luke 2:8–14).

Anything but Turnips

One of our New Year's Eve traditions when I was growing up was inviting family members to our house for a party. Living out in the country, you could shoot fireworks and bang pots and pans without bothering your neighbors. Kids ran all over the place while adults kicked back and did what adults do best—telling kids to slow down and quit slamming doors.

One particular year we had received a big box of turnips just prior to the holidays. When I say a big box, I would estimate about fifty pounds. Now I can eat most anything you put in front of me, but turnips are not one of those items. I was forced to try them on several occasions but for some reason they instantly engaged my gag reflex. Back in the day you ate what was served or you didn't eat. It never even entered my mind to ask my mom to prepare another meal just for me. A request like that would have invoked "the look" from my father that closely resembled burning laser beams of hot magma along with the message "Have you lost your mind?" There was no alternative meal choice if you were not keen on the main dish.

So here we are celebrating New Year's Eve, kids running everywhere and adults consuming coffee by the gallon. As we approached midnight I was running out of steam. Before long I passed out on the couch. I don't know exactly what happened next, but my sister tells the story with great detail. Since she's my sister, I believe the story has been embellished extensively over the years. Apparently I rose from my sleeping place on the couch and walked into the kitchen. By divine providence or an honest mistake by a sleepwalking kid, I apparently thought I was in the bathroom. I dropped my drawers in front of a kitchen full of women and cut loose on the box of turnips. According to witnesses I must have drunk quite a bit of pop that night because it went on for a while. I was definitely in a deep sleep because the screams from those present never pierced my consciousness. I pulled up my drawers, walked back to the front room, and returned to my sleeping place on the couch.

I've always wondered if God didn't have something to do with that episode. I know I had said a prayer when I saw that box of turnips show up. I also believe that God listens to the prayers of kids. We adults might think they are silly or cute. I think God finds them powerful. I've been thinking about all the kids who are praying for my son. I equate their prayers with the most mighty of prayer warriors. I can hardly catch my breath when I think about the life lesson that will be engraved in their hearts when Hudson walks again. Since I know God has a great sense of humor, I wouldn't be surprised if it turns out to be a sleepwalking episode. I wonder where I could get a box of turnips.

> *Whoever fears the Lord has a secure fortress,*
> *and for their children it will be a refuge*
> (Proverbs 14:26).

8

Hide and Seek

My mom is a saint. Let me make that point right from the start. For her to have put up with me all these years, I can only imagine the number of jewels in her crown when she gets to heaven. I was the high-energy type of child who seemed to go nonstop. That did not go well with the expectations placed upon me when we went to church. To put a kid through an hour of Sunday School and then a two-hour worship service was, in my opinion at the time, completely unfair.

My typical Sunday went something like this. Get up, eat three bowls of Rice Krispies with at least sixteen spoonsful of sugar in each bowl, and watch "Davey and Goliath." I would then start getting ready for church, which always involved searching for my "church" shoes for thirty minutes. We would then do the three-hour church gig. During the service I would get "the look" from my mom several times. That was followed by the "Wait until I tell your father" speech on the way home.

Once home, I would assume the position and get my booty busted. I would then do it all over again for the evening service.

For the record, I deserved every one of those "beatings." A word of advice here. Don't threaten your parents with calling the child abuse hotline just prior to an "attitude adjustment." Just saying. My parents tried their best to teach me the way I should go. I was blessed beyond measure by my parents. It wasn't until I had my own kids that I truly understood the love Tim and Virginia Haws had for me.

It became very clear one day in the early 90s. My oldest son, Jackson, was around three years old. We were at an apparel store shopping for some clothes. When it was time to check out, Jackson wasn't at my side. I looked around and could not find him. I looked harder. Nothing. It got to the point that I became frantic, and I told the manager that no one was to leave the store. I began calling Jackson's name as loud as I could. Nothing. Then out of the corner of my eye I saw some clothes move. As I approached the rack, I found Jackson hiding in the center of it. He thought we were playing hide-and-seek. The relief was overwhelming! Our lost son was found!

God knows a lot about searching for lost children. Just as finding Jackson completely focused my attention that day, I believe God is intently focused on seeking and saving the lost. Maybe He's even using Hudson's situation, or one you are going through, to get your attention. Maybe this ordeal is the search-and-rescue flare God is using to get you to grab His hand, to bring you back into the fold. If that's the case, we praise God and rejoice in the expansion of His kingdom!

*Jesus entered Jericho and was passing through.
A man was there by the name of Zacchaeus; he was a
chief tax collector and was wealthy. He wanted to see who
Jesus was, but because he was short he could not see over the
crowd. So he ran ahead and climbed a sycamore-fig tree to see
him, since Jesus was coming that way. When Jesus reached the
spot, he looked up and said to him, "Zacchaeus, come down immediately. I must stay at your house today." So he came down at
once and welcomed him gladly. All the people saw this and began
to mutter, "He has gone to be the guest of a sinner." But Zacchaeus stood up and said to the Lord, "Look, Lord! Here and now
I give half of my possessions to the poor, and if I have cheated
anybody out of anything, I will pay back four times the
amount." Jesus said to him, "Today salvation has come to
this house, because this man, too, is a son of Abraham.
For the Son of Man came to seek and to save the lost"*
(Luke 19:1–10).

9

Four Faithful Friends

It was Easter weekend and our pastor was speaking about miracles. He talked about a few other things, but to tell you the truth I focused on the miracle section. I know a kid who needs one of those. The whole weekend reminded me of a miracle Jesus performed just after He called His disciples.

Jesus was in a home teaching. The place was packed. It was so full of people that they were spilling out the front door. Then four guys show up carrying a paralyzed man. All five of these guys remain nameless. For all we know, this is their only reference in the Bible. Yet somehow I feel that I know these guys.

I can definitely relate to the guy on the mat. I wonder if he was eighteen and hurt in a chariot race or wrestling match. I wonder what kind of blood pressure, skin, bowel, and bladder issues he suffered. I imagine he had scored an A on the Asia Scale and that the local healers had determined his injury complete. I bet those same healers looked him in the eye and told him he would never walk again. I know he was scared. The kid was on an emotional roller coaster.

I also know this young man was loved. He had four friends who were givers. I know exactly the type of guys they were. They spent their time and efforts making sure their friend was doing okay. They spent nights right after he was injured making sure his house would accommodate his needs. They went all out, no skimping or shortcuts. Even though a couple lived out of town, they made frequent trips to check on their hurt friend. They even hauled extra people with them because they knew it would boost his spirits.

One of the guys really didn't know the hurt guy that well. But he was a giver. He had kids of his own and could only imagine what the family was going through. He was local so any "out of towners" were welcomed to stay in his home. He fed many a stranger and spent hours going out of his way for the sake of a hurt kid.

These guys would come over after work or school and hang out with this kid. They would pick him up and carry him around with them so he could get out of his house. Some of the friends were married. Their wives organized meals to be delivered to the kid's house. They put him on all their scroll study prayer lists.

Then word began to spread about this man named Jesus. People were telling fantastic stories of healing. Lepers, demon-possessed, blind, and lame were being restored. Jesus was having to move around quite a bit in order to keep from getting swarmed by the crowds. Sometimes He went out into the wilderness just to get some alone time. There were a lot of parents watching, waiting, desperate to hear if He were close.

The four guys were also waiting and watching. They had a plan. Then the news arrived. Jesus had arrived in Capernaum. They dropped everything. Jobs and classes were left behind. Camels were left to wander, reins still in the ignition. "The plan" was a go. They grabbed a corner of their friend's mat and headed toward Capernaum.

They were looking for a house off Main Street on the west edge of town. As they approached, their hearts sank for a moment. People were everywhere. They couldn't even see this Jesus, much less the front door. They began assessing the situation. I'm sure they heard whispers in their soul: "You heard what the doctors said—*complete.* You guys are going to be the laughingstock of the town. He isn't healing—He's teaching. It's going to take too much time. This kid just needs to accept that this is what God wants for his life." But they were determined. They believed. If there was a chance this Jesus could help their friend, they were going to see it through.

Then someone spotted the roof and Plan B was implemented. They ignored the guy who told them they couldn't go up there. The four began working fast. When they had left the house the need for tools wasn't on their mind. Thankfully they found a length of rope. The roof was rock-hard mud tiles and they needed to create a hole. They made a quick estimate where the access point should be located. Then the whispers started again: "This is going to cost you a lot of money in repairs. This Jesus is too busy. The kid doesn't even profess a close walk with God. This is going to be embarrassing. You're digging in the wrong place." Again they didn't listen. Instead—they dug.

The sharp edges of the tiles bit into their hands. They looked for handholds to pull in order to loosen the layers. The sound of muffled voices reached their ears as they removed roofing inch by inch. The muffled voices soon turned into cries of displeasure from the crowd inside the house as hardened mud and dust pelted them from above. The digging grew to a frenzy as the first signs of light greeted the excavators. They soon had a hole big enough to see into the house. And that's when they saw Him.

Jesus hadn't moved. He dusted off some tile fragments from his beard and looked intently at the four faces staring at Him from above. The four faces disappeared and soon a wobbling mat began floating down toward the crowd in the house. The kid's mat settled onto the floor at the feet of Jesus. Their eyes meet. Jesus glanced back at the four faces that had reappeared in the hole above.

His next statement shocked everyone: "Son, your sins are forgiven." The four friends take pause. "What did He say?" The crowd inside the house began to grumble, especially the teachers of the Law. "Who does this guy think He is?" Everyone was debating the words Jesus spoke—everyone but a kid on a mat. He couldn't say a word because the enormous weight, the chains that had gripped his soul, had just fallen off.

The kid had showed up with hopes of walking again. How many times had he dreamed of running again, fishing with his buddies, or spending time at hunting camp? His friends were so excited when they told him the news of this Jesus. The flame of hope was ignited once again. But he wasn't expecting this newfound freedom. Just as he had forgotten what it felt like to walk, he had also forgotten what it felt like to be guilt free.

Then Jesus rose and started speaking. The whole place fell into a hushed silence. He appeared to know exactly what everyone had been saying under their breaths. Jesus said, "Why are you thinking these things? Which is easier: to say to this paralyzed man, 'Your sins are forgiven,' or to say, 'Get up, take your mat and walk'? But I want you to know that the Son of Man has authority on earth to forgive sins" (Mark 2:8–10).

The kid on the mat couldn't take his eyes off Jesus. Then the young man heard the words "I tell you, get up, take up your mat and go home" (v. 11). Another weight was lifted. It was the ten-thousand-pound blanket that had been covering his body from his chest down since his injury.

Neurons began to fire. His legs began moving. It wasn't a muscle spasm this time. It wasn't a reflex. His hands straightened out on demand. He could wiggle his fingers and toes. All of a sudden he felt the urge to go to the bathroom. He could feel the electrical impulses moving through his leg muscles. The young man jumped to his feet, feeling power surge through his body. No blood pressure issues, no atrophied muscles, everything working just as it did the day he was born. He was healed from head to toe.

The kid walks over, looks Jesus in the eye, and says, "Thank you." He gives Jesus a hug, then scoops up his mat and walks out the front door, where he is mauled by four excited friends. The whole place is amazed and people break out in songs of praise.

The Bible tells us that Jesus saw the faith of the four friends. As I sat in church on Easter, I was reminded of our faithful friends. Keeping the faith, lifting our son to Jesus, every single day. Friends who haven't given up, they don't listen to the whispers—they are keeping the faith. Thank you, "givers" of the world! We are blessed with faithful friends and an amazing God.

You are the God who performs miracles;
you display your power among the peoples
(Psalm 77:14).

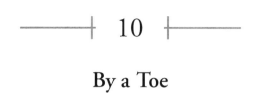

By a Toe

In December 1979 my dad and uncle decided to go on a pheasant hunting trip in Nebraska. I got to tag along. I don't remember much about the trip out because like most teenagers, I slept the whole way. When I woke up we were in Red Cloud, Nebraska.

Our first day of hunting was awesome. It was mild and sunny and pheasants were everywhere. My dad and uncle limited out quickly. I, on the other hand, couldn't hit the broad side of a barn. It was the most pathetic display of shooting I had ever seen, if I say so myself. After what had to be my seventy-eighth missed shot, my dad and uncle couldn't contain themselves any longer. The trash talking commenced, comments like "Are you sure you're not shooting your BB gun?" or "That last shot was really close—I actually mistook you for a hunter." By the end of the day I was skunked. I went to bed determined to redeem myself.

When we woke the next morning the landscape had changed. A storm had moved in overnight and now there was six inches of snow on the ground and the wind was howling. The temperature was near zero and the windchill close to forty below. We went to the local diner to eat breakfast and rethink our strategy. I will never forget looking out the front window of the diner and watching a Harley Davidson motorcycle appear through the haze of the blizzard. A huge man got off the bike and walked in to the greetings of many of the patrons. It turns out that he was the town priest. I was impressed.

After breakfast we decided to head out and give the pheasants a try. To say it was cold was an understatement. The first stop produced no birds but I could have sworn my fingers were frozen solid. As we drove down the road we spotted a bunch of birds running around by an old barn. We parked and walked the lane toward the scurrying birds. Pheasants were everywhere. I thought my time had come. The birds were just about to flush when all of a sudden a bald eagle swooped in and snagged a fleeing meal. I just stood there in awe. That was the first bald eagle I had seen in the wild. I think it gave me a little look over its shoulder that said, "That's how it's done."

We went back to the truck and headed to our next stop. Still without a bird to my name, I was eager to get another chance. Suddenly my dad pulled over and pointed out a rooster pheasant in the corner of a nearby field. I got out and stalked within range. I believe the bird was frozen in place or blind because it did not move. It's not legal to shoot a game bird on the ground. Let's just say I barely let that pheasant get his toe-nail clear of the dirt before I cut loose. The bird collapsed and I retrieved my prize. I put the pheasant in the back of the SUV and tried to warm up.

I began bragging as we drove down the road about how it had taken me one only shot to down that bird. No sooner had I gotten that out of my mouth than the pheasant poked his head up over the back seat. This rooster then decided he didn't like what he saw and was going to make a break for it. He began flying around in the truck making loud squawking sounds while we dove for cover. My dad got the truck pulled over and I bailed out just in time to see my "prize" spring from the cab and sail off into the Nebraska blue yonder. I remember my uncle looking at me and saying, "One shot?"

My shooting did improve and we had a great week—capped off by a Sooner win over Nebraska in the 1979 Orange Bowl. We watched the game in a Kansas hotel room just in case our cheering got out of control.

There have been stretches of time in my spiritual life that I couldn't hit the proverbial broad side of a barn. Despite my best aim I kept missing the mark. But just like my earthly father, who kept handing me box after box of ammo, our Heavenly Father isn't keeping score. I think He delights in the fact that we keep on shooting for the mark. God doesn't wait until we are sharpshooters. In fact, we hit the bull's-eye when we allow Him to take control. I also love the fact that when we think it's over, when we believe hope is completely dead, miraculous things happen! A dead neuron can spring back to life. A blocked pathway can become clear. Electrical impulses can fly into nerve centers. God swoops in like an eagle and shows us how it is done. The cheering will be out of control!

Because of his great love for us, God, who is rich in mercy, made us alive with Christ even when we were dead in transgressions—it is by grace you have been saved (Ephesians 2:4–5).

11

Mud Pies

I went to the eye doctor yesterday. He confirmed that I'm almost as blind as a bat. I'm blessed with the miracle of glasses and contact lenses to keep my sight as clear as possible. My vision corrects well with the right prescription. In fact, I found myself feeling pretty sure of myself as I read the eye chart with my glasses or contacts. I was reading those really small lines until I was asked to remove my glasses. I don't think I could have read the first big line. Again, I'm thankful for the tools we have to help us see better.

Vision is such a wonderful gift from God. To witness a sunrise or sunset, to watch the world around us blossom as spring arrives, or to marvel at the athletic ability within March Madness is a huge blessing. When I read about the blind man in John 9, I'm intrigued by the story. It starts off with the question to Jesus about why the man was born blind. "Was this man born blind because of *his* sin or his *parents'* sin?"

I've always thought that was a crazy question until recently. I have to admit that when someone you love is suffering, you start doing inventory. Has one of us done something to upset God? Are we not praying enough? Do we have things out of whack in our relationship with God? I think Satan uses tough situations to hammer us with doubt and guilt.

I take comfort when Jesus rejects either option and says, "Neither." Then He does something crazy. He begins spitting in the dirt and making some mud. He then takes the mud and puts it on the blind man's eyes. Jesus could have just said a word, nodded His head, even thought the thought and the man would be healed. Why all the mud pie stuff?

Growing up, I got dirty a lot. The dirt at our place was about as red as it could get. I can remember times when the bottom of the bathtub was solid red dirt. My mom fought the good fight trying to keep us kids clean. The worst job we had was to clean the dirt off the walls of our house. Living in a log cabin, my mom would periodically have us wipe down the logs. I loathed the job for some reason. It was monotonous and our house seemed to double in square footage when it was time to clean the walls.

I'm not a big fan of dirt. I'm even less a fan of spit. My mom wasn't a fan either. Any spitting was a sure-fire way to get lit up when dad got home. The expectation was clear: keep your spit in your mouth. My sister would occasionally ignore the spit rule when she was solidifying her rank as number-one kid. She would tackle one of us, pin our arms down with her knees, and then act as if she were going to spit in our face. Sometimes she would let the spit start to drop toward our face before she would slurp it back into her mouth. Every once in a while she didn't slurp very well and we got a face full of spit. It was as gross as it sounds.

Spit grosses me out big time. I don't even like my own spit unless it's in my mouth. I remember times when guys would spit into a cup and then dare people to drink it. I wouldn't have done it for a million bucks—even if it were my own spit. No way.

So here we have Jesus taking two things a lot of people don't like, dirt and spit, and rubs them on a blind man's eyes. I can only imagine what the blind guy was thinking. I'm sure the crowd was reacting to the spit-and-dirt application to the man's eyes. Is this Jesus guy making a mockery of me? I didn't ask Him to do this. Then after his eyes are pasted with spit mud, Jesus tells him to go wash in the pool of Siloam. He doesn't take the guy there. He doesn't send a disciple with him to the pool. He tells the blind guy to find his way to the pool on his own, eyes coated with mud. To the man's credit, he goes, washes, and regains his sight. I have no doubt he was seeing better than 20/20.

I love this story because it reminds me that Jesus can take the most basic of stuff, dirt, and turn it into something miraculous. He can take things that appall us, spit, and use it to restore. Jesus is in the restoration business.

Feel like dirt sometimes? Appalled at some of the things you do? Jesus knows all about it. You are never too dirty, never too appalling for Jesus. He can take whatever you bring to Him and make it new.

After you have suffered a little while,
the God of all grace, who has called you to
his eternal glory in Christ, will himself restore,
confirm, strengthen, and establish you
(1 Peter 5:10 ESV).

12

Gone in Sixty Seconds

Every summer throughout my college career I worked night shift for a well-known ice cream company in Oklahoma. My best friend's dad was the CFO and had put in a good word for me. I was hired on at the processing plant.

I'll never forget my first day on the job. I was introduced to the dock foreman and he immediately put me to work. He asked if I had ever run a forklift. It just so happens that I had. He told me to go pick up a big plastic tub of top-secret ingredients and take it to the ice cream production room. I jumped onto the forklift and proceeded toward two giant plastic tubs. One was stacked on top of the other. The side of the tub cautioned amateurs that the contents weighed approximately five hundred pounds.

I whipped the lift around, aimed the forks toward the slots, and began hoisting the tub skyward. What I didn't know was that the forklift had just come out of the freezer and the metal was as slick as ice. As I lifted the tub, my forks were ever so slightly slanted downward. That's all it took for gravity to take over. The tub slid off the forks, clipped the tub below, and I got to see five hundred pounds of cookies fly down the docking bay.

My first thought was inappropriate. My second thought was "Hey—those are the cookies they use for cookies and cream ice cream!" My third thought was "I'm going to be the fastest person ever fired at this company." The foreman came running, saw the avalanche of cookies spread across the dock, and began pulling freight boxes over to block the view. He then told me that it would be a really good idea if I got those cookies swept off the dock before the plant manager saw the mess.

I set a new world record for cookie sweeping that day and made friends with all the local raccoons. Every evening when I came to work I would see herds of raccoons outside the dock doors gorging themselves on cookies. Needless to say, I wasn't fired and worked many shifts at the plant. My main job was working in the freezer where they stored ice cream. I wore an outfit that looked perfect if you were on an expedition to the North Pole. It looked super weird to wear it to work in the middle of an Oklahoma summer.

It was my task to keep the metal roller beds, which held newly filled containers of ice cream, empty so that ice cream production could continue. It was made crystal clear to me by the plant manager that if I did not keep the area empty, causing ice cream production to stop because of said failure, then my lucrative career there would come to an end.

The freezer, which served as my office, was kept at -27 degrees Fahrenheit. This did not take into account the wind chill created by the huge fans that blew across the metal roller beds where the ice cream was sent to freeze. I worked mainly by myself. I had a counterpart in the freezer next door who was busy following the same mandate I had received from the manager. We would visit on breaks and help each other if there was a rare problem.

I received a quick tutorial my first day on how to operate the machinery. There were some warnings about hypothermia and death but when you're in your twenties those elude your thought process. Then there were the things no one told you about. For instance, did you know that one of the main coolants used in refrigeration is ammonia? And did you know that when there is an ammonia leak you can't see or breathe?

But what I wasn't expecting was the first time my eyes froze shut. When I was working fast and breathing hard, my breath would saturate my eyelashes, which would then quickly freeze together. The first time it happened I freaked out. I had huge mittens on my hands and couldn't figure out what was going on. I had to walk my way out by memory. Once outside I could take off my gloves and hold my eyelashes until the ice melted and my eyes would open.

Lisa and I have had to make a lot of decisions about Hudson and his care. The number of things you need to care for chronically injured people is staggering. There are so many items you don't naturally think about but may potentially need. I am here to testify that throughout the process we have not been stumbling around with our eyes frozen shut. We are not staggering around trying to find our way. Why? Because God is faithful. His Word says, "Whether you turn to the right or to the left, your ears will hear a voice behind you, saying, 'This is the way; walk in it'" (Isaiah 30:21).

God has blessed us with members of His kingdom who continue to shower us with support. He has lived up to His promise to strengthen us and help us. We have been upheld by His righteous right hand. We will continue to ask for God's wisdom and seek His guidance. He knows the way!

If any of you lacks wisdom, you should ask God,
who gives generously to all without finding fault,
and it will be given to you
(James 1:5).

13

How Can It Be?

I don't know about you, but as a kid I spent a lot of time in trouble. Typically I would go a stretch of days happy and carefree. But once the wheels started coming off the wagon, it usually took a while to work my way back into the good graces of my parents. It's not that they held a grudge—I would just keep making poor choices. Sometimes I was sentenced to my bedroom. Occasionally I got a stern talking-to from one or both parents. Most of the time I got to "ride the lightning." My parents didn't beat me, but they would dish out swift and attention-getting punishment in the form of a spanking.

My mom tried her best, but most of the time we were dodging blows and dancing around, which made it hard on her. I had to be careful, though. If I didn't let mom dish out consequences to her satisfaction, I had to deal with Dad. My dad could take care of business. He was a big guy and had excellent hand-eye coordination.

If I attempted to dance around the blow, I was hoisted into the air with my legs dangling like a marionette doll. He would then use my momentum against me. As I recoiled from swat #1, he would catch me on the downfall and use the laws of physics to his advantage.

I don't remember my sister getting more than one or two spankings in her life. I would like to credit that to the fact that she was the golden child. I actually think it's due to the fact that she was a great kid and smarter than I was. Plus, my siblings could blame most anything on me, and my parents usually bought it. I don't blame them.

I became an expert on reading my parents and riding the line between a "talking-to" and Swatsville. Some days I misjudged. I deserved every spanking I got and should have received many more. Sure, I took a few that should have gone to a sibling, but it all evened out in the wash.

My worst thrashing occurred on what should have been a glorious day. My dad had taken my brother and me fishing. We were out in the middle of nowhere at a farm pond near our grandparents' house, so Grandpa was with us. The fish were not cooperating. As a kid with ADHD, it took me about twenty casts, and I was distracted.

After about an hour in hot and windy conditions, I was tired of not catching a fish. I decided to ask my dad for the car keys so I could sit and listen to the radio. I made the trek to the far side of the pond where my dad and grandpa were fishing and pled my case for the car keys; my dad obliged. He did warn me about four times not to lock the keys in the car. I was like "I'm not an idiot, Dad. The keys are safe with me." My brother caught on to my plan and decided to tag along.

As we neared the car, I took off running. I made it to the driver-side door first, so I jumped in and quickly locked the doors. I turned on the radio and began to tease my brother. I would unlock a door, tell him to come on around and get in, then lock it right before he opened the door. I kept that up for a good ten minutes before I realized how hot it was getting in the car. I couldn't roll down the window or my brother would enter my kingdom. It came to a point where the car became too hot and I decided to end the unlock/lock game.

When my brother jumped into the car, I decided to go fish some more. I told him to make sure he didn't leave the keys in the car and headed to the pond. Five minutes later, he came running up to me with his fishing pole in hand. I asked him for the car keys. He didn't have them. I dropped my pole and ran to the car. The door was locked. The fear and panic rose as I tried each door to no avail. They were all locked. I plastered my face against the driver window and could see the keys lying on the seat. Then I looked from there through the front windshield and saw my dad and grandpa slowly making their way back from the far side of the pond.

Back in those days cars were made of steel—not the plastic or aluminum cars of today—good ol' American steel. I put it to the test as I pulled on the car handles with all my might. At one point I had hold of the driver-side handle with both feet on the car door. Nothing budged. I tried the little side windows. Locked. As my dad and grandpa edged closer and closer, I could hear his words echo in my mind: "Do *not* lock the keys in the car."

Of all the things that could happen, we had done the one thing forbidden by my dad. The word *idiot* kept rolling over and over in my mind. As my dad walked up, he asked me for the keys. I then proceeded to throw my brother completely under the bus. I even got behind him and gently threw him toward my father in sacrifice for our transgression. That little move proved to be a mistake because I got to see what was in store for me.

Needless to say, I got it, and I mean good. When the dust began to settle, my dad started walking off. I was sad because I thought he was going to walk miles to find help. Instead, he soon turned around and headed back for us. I was preparing myself for round two of the "Don't be an idiot" lesson. This time my dad had a long piece of metal wire in his hand. I was like "Holy smokes—we *are* gonna die!" My dad took the wire, wedged it between the window and the car frame, and had the vehicle unlocked in about seven seconds. At first I was relieved that we weren't going to have a round two; then I was mad that I had to take a beating for something so easily remedied.

I would like to say that I never locked the keys in the car again. I wish this were the story of my worst transgression to date. I can't claim any of those things. There was a point in my life when I could relate to the first few lines of Lauren Daigle's song "How Can It Be." She sings about our guilt and the shame we feel about all the ugly mess we make of our lives. Many times we just want to hide the numerous ways in which we've let God down. We doubt His love for us. When tragedy strikes, we figure that it's just punishment for not measuring up.

I don't think God works that way. I remember those days when I carried the weight of sin—guilty, deserving of judgment and punishment. Then Jesus finally got my attention. I unlocked the door of my heart and let Him in. The chains of sin fell off, and I was free. The punishment I deserved was now replaced with only grace. And as Ms. Daigle's song says, Jesus pleads our cause and rights our wrongs. It's an undeserved act of grace.

I still shake my head in wonder at the gift of grace Jesus, my Savior, has given me. It doesn't add up. It has never added up. Jesus has always given more than I ever could repay. Life instead of death, mercy in lieu of wrath, love in place of punishment. How can it be? He loves us!

Let us then with confidence draw near to
the throne of grace, that we may receive mercy and
find grace to help in time of need
(Hebrews 4:16 ESV).

Bringing the Heat

Hudson is constantly battling body temperature and blood pressure issues. It's getting better at times. It's weird watching him sweat like crazy yet be freezing at the same time.

I know a few things about being cold. When I was young, my family lived in a log cabin. I don't say that figuratively. We lived in a house made of logs and mortar. We could literally climb the walls. Where the logs intersected, the ends would stick out a foot or two from floor to ceiling. I climbed up those natural ladders countless times as a kid. I guess you could say that our house was both a home and a big play toy.

Unfortunately, our home was not well insulated. I remember waking up on winter mornings and it being so cold in my bedroom that I could see my breath. Since our parents didn't believe in using the heater, we were highly encouraged to layer up in clothing. The only problem with layering was that we had only two sets of clothes. If we didn't get our own laundry done, we just had to tough it out. My brother and I would share the one blanket we were allotted unless my sister was willing to part with one of her six or seven blankets for a night. On very cold nights my brother and I would sneak out to the car, start it up, and sleep with the heater on full blast. We then had to sneak back in before my folks woke up or we would take a beating. Ok, I have to stop. I made all that stuff up just to get my mom worked up. I know she's reading this and I figured she needed a good "Oh, my goodness" moment.

We did live in a log cabin. That part is true, along with the fact it wasn't well insulated. In fact, I could see the trees outside my room through cracks in my bedroom wall. The rule of the house was that the first person up in the morning had to light the gas stove in the bathroom. I spent many a cold morning with my blanket draped over me "tent style" in order to catch every bit of heat the stove put out. Sometimes I would lock the door to the bathroom so I could selfishly hog the heat. My brother and sister would bang on the bathroom door, wanting in to get warmed up. The banging didn't last long. Our bathroom doorknob could be picked in like two seconds.

One particular Sunday morning the Haws kids were jockeying for heater space before we had to head out for church. My sister had the front-and-center section pretty-much secured and was effectively boxing out my brother and me. Unfortunately for her, the dress she was wearing caught fire. My brother and I put our lives on the line, disregarded our own personal safety, and extinguished the flames as if we belonged on the show *Emergency!* My sister is also reading this, so I must confess that I probably embellished that a little too. She got the burning dress off quickly and averted injury.

The warmth and light from the little stove brought us so much comfort over the years. It drew us in over and over. We knew where to go on a cold morning when we needed a little extra heat. When I was in college and struggling with my relationship with God, I believe the prayers of my mom and all those Sunday School lessons, sermons, hymns, church camps, youth retreats, scriptures, and revivals called to me like a warm stove on a cold morning. When I had questions, the seed of faith that had been planted began producing a harvest. I'm not questioning the faith of my Sunday School teachers, but I'm sure a couple were shocked that God was able to get me to hear His call. When my soul was cold and dark, in need of a Savior, I called to Him. The spark was lit. The warmth and light of a loving Father radiated through my soul. Got someone for whom you've been praying for a long time? Don't give up! Got a kid you know who is driving you crazy? Keep planting those seeds. Jesus will keep knocking on the door of his or her heart, calling to the kid like a warm stove on a cold morning. I pray he or she will open the door.

We are able to hold our heads high no matter what happens and know that all is well, for we know how dearly God loves us, and we feel this warm love everywhere within us because God has given us the Holy Spirit to fill our hearts with his love
(Romans 5:5 TLB).

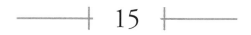

15

He's Not Heavy

My grandparents on my dad's side had a farmhouse north of Crescent, Oklahoma. They officially lived out in the middle of nowhere. We made the hour drive countless times over the years.

It's interesting what you remember about a place you frequented as a child. I remember how red the dirt roads leading to their house were and that if you hit the railroad crossing at forty miles per hour your stomach would drop. The hand pump you had to use to get water into the bathtub was mesmerizing as a child. The rotten egg fights we had in the barn were instant classics. I remember that the best place to dig for worms was near the hen house. I can still almost taste the merengue from the pies my grandma would have waiting for dessert.

I remember that we were not going to leave until after the television comedy *Hee Haw* was over. We would then load up and head home. Back in those days we had no idea about seat belts. Each of us had his or her own place on the way home. My sister got the entire back seat, so that left one of two places for my brother and me. We would choose anywhere from the floorboard or the space between the back seats and the back window of the car. I usually chose the back window. I loved staring up through the window at the countless stars. Away from the city lights the sky seemed to teem with galaxy after galaxy.

We usually didn't make it too far down the road before I was asleep, and I would wake up when my dad was carrying me into the house. However, sometimes if I were awake when we pulled into the driveway, I would fake asleep. I loved it when my dad carried me in and put me into my bed. It was so comforting being in the arms of my father.

Recently there have been times when I wish I could fall asleep and wake up to find that this is all just a big nightmare. I'm sure Hudson has felt the same way. He told me the other day that he dreams of running with his buddies. Throughout this ordeal I have felt God's comforting arms around me and my family.

As I look back, I know the only way we have made it this far is because He has carried us. We begin another week of therapy knowing that God will carry us through day by day. I look forward to the stories I will get to tell my grandchildren about the time God carried us while we were going through rough times. Those are already gearing up to be some for the ages!

The eternal God is your refuge,
and underneath are the everlasting arms
(Deuteronomy 33:27).

16

Mom's Gift

I'm a music lover. There's something about music that allows me to think and work better. I'm not exclusive to any particular genre. Most of the time I listen to the music that I grew up hearing on the radio. Growing up during the 60s, 70s, and 80s opened the door to quite the diversity in tunes. I'm sure the people I work with shake their heads in amazement at the songs that come floating out of my office— from Glenn Campbell's "Wichita Lineman" and Rush's "Red Barchetta" to tunes by the O'Jays, The Four Seasons, Elvis Presley, and Dan Fogelberg. George Jones is in my library as well The Jackson 5. I can crank Journey as well as Kenny Chesney.

I can also rock out to Led Zeppelin or dance to the Bee Gees. Okay, I don't dance, but I could put John Travolta to shame if I wanted to! The London Philharmonic Orchestra is available and so is Madonna. I can try to sing along with Mary J. Blige or Night Ranger. I can jam to the guitar riffs of Peter Frampton and Eddie Van Halen or admire the harmony of Simon & Garfunkel. I have let the sunshine in more than once listening to The 5th Dimension.

My love for music begins with my mom. Her passion for music spilled over into her children. The Haws kids were regulars on the Sunday night lineup at church. We could belt out a pretty good version of "I'll Fly Away" if I don't say so myself. I thank my mom for the gift of music that I enjoy today. It has been a lifelong blessing.

Ever since the day of Hudson's injury, music has ministered to me in a special way. Not any of the songs by The Who or U2. I haven't played any Boston or Pink Floyd. My soul has yearned for those songs that remind me of God and His character. I have been wearing out Jeremy Camp and Steven Curtis Chapman. Mandisa and the Newsboys are cued up regularly. Michael W. Smith and MercyMe could have their own playlist.

Much to Hudson's chagrin, I am binge-playing Christmas tunes right now. I guess the versions I like don't fit his personality. I think if I play "Veni, Veni," by Mannheim Steamroller one more time he is going to start throwing things at me. But I can't help it. My soul is crying out, "O come, O come, Emmanuel. . . ." Sorry, Hudson, but I think I just hit the "loop" button.

I will sing to the Lord as long as I live;
I will sing praise to my God while I have being
(Psalm 104:33 NKJV).

17

Not Feeling the Sting

Growing up out in the country, you have to put up with your share of bugs. We had tons of red ants that I waged war against every Fourth of July. They were armed with their mandibles and I with my Black Cat firecrackers. I carpet bombed their "bed" until I ran out of ordnance. We also had to deal with scorpions. I tried to stay away from those bad boys. I'll never forget the worker on a nearby farm who was stung on the hand by a scorpion. It was as though someone had pumped about twenty-five pounds of air into his hand.

Thankfully, I've never been stung by a scorpion. They have crawled across my chest, feet, and legs but never lit me up. I've been stung by many a wasp and bee in my life. I remember the first time I ever got stung. I was chasing my sister with a baseball bat. I don't recall what no-good, low-down, big-sister thing she did to me, but it had to be bad. She ran for cover behind some shrubs next to the house. I began thrashing the shrubs with my bat. The yellow jacket in the shrub took offense and came after me. I got a close-up view of the whole thing since it stung me right next to my eye. It landed on my face, pulled its stinger up and licked it, then plunged it about three feet deep into my cheek. From that point on I fought a fear of bees and wasps.

At any given time during the summer, we would have a wasp or two flying around inside our home. It was like getting strafed by a Japanese Zero. I would dive for cover and then run for the hills. They were usually just mud daubers but since they flew and had a stinger, I took no chances. Our homestead was ripe for wasp nests. We had several barns that provided prime spots for big wasp condos. Every once in a while we would have to battle some red wasps. They like to swarm at people in big numbers. They can build some big nests and absolutely don't like visitors.

Yellow jackets, of course, were the ones I hated. They would release some sort of pheromone that painted you like a laser for a rocket launcher. Once they got you with that stuff, the others would home in on you and the battle was on. Then you had the head honchos, the bumblebees. I feared bumblebees more than anything else, especially when I found out that they can sting you over and over. We got a big nest of those in our barn once, and they wouldn't let us within fifty feet of the barn door. We pulled the old half-full plastic bottle trick on them. If you have never seen how that works, you should look it up on You-Tube—an easy way to get rid of those black-and-yellow beasts without getting throttled.

No matter how careful I was, I usually got smoked by a bee or wasp several times a year. One time I was stung while driving a truck loaded with lumber. The bee flew in through the open window and drilled me in the cheek. It was just a honeybee, but it was the first time I had really experienced an allergic reaction. About six years ago I got stung at the base of my skull near my hairline by a yellow jacket. I ended up in the emergency room needing a big shot of Benadryl. I now really have to watch getting stung because of the allergic reaction issues. It's not the pain of the sting—it's the reaction to the sting that could possibly kill me.

The worst insect attack I have ever faced came on a hot summer day. My friend Steve and I were hot and sweaty from mowing and looking for a way to cool off. His neighbors had a pool that was calling our names. We decided to hop their fence, take a quick dip in the pool, and go on with our day. As if it were destiny, the neighbors left on cue and we proceeded to crawl over the fence.

Halfway over the gate, it opened with me straddling the top. I made some statement about us being intellectual giants and then hopped down. That's when the first three wasps nailed me. Before I could register exactly what was happening, two more found their target. I took off running. I bee-lined (no pun intended) to the pool and dove into the deep end. I could see the swarm dive bombing the top of the water, waiting for me to reappear. I set a new unofficial world record for holding one's breath that day. Once I got the nerve to emerge from the pool, we discovered a huge red wasp nest in the gate. It worked better than a junkyard dog for the rest of the summer—we never hopped their fence again.

I'm reminded that there are things worse than the sting or attack of an insect. When I became a father, my focus shifted to the mental and physical safety of my kids. As a Christian parent, I pray for their salvation. I believe their souls are going to live forever. The place of their future dwelling will be based on whether they have received the gift of salvation offered through Jesus.

If I could make that choice for my sons, it would have been done the moment they entered this world. I pray my sons will always walk with the Lord. I try to set an example that would show them Jesus. Ultimately, I don't get to make the decision for them and that is scary for me. It's hard for parents to watch their kids make poor choices. It stings worse than any bumblebee could dish out.

Scripture tells us about the sting of death—sin. The venom of sin runs in our veins looking to kill and destroy. It was in my sons' veins from their first cries. The great news is that we have the ultimate anti-venom. The solution to the problem of sin is before each of us. We can't hide from sin. We can't "man up." Our parents or loved ones can't take it away from us. But we have a Savior who can. Our victory is through Jesus Christ. We don't have to run for cover, dive for safety, or even fear the sting. Because of Him we can say, "Where, O death, is your victory? Where, O death, is your sting?" (1 Corinthians 15:55). The tomb is empty! Praise be to Jesus Christ, the Son of the living God. He has conquered death!

> *He will wipe away every tear from their eyes,*
> *and death shall be no more, neither shall there be*
> *mourning, nor crying, nor pain anymore, for the*
> *former things have passed away*
> (Revelation 21:4 ESV).

Reversals

As we have grown older, our Fourth of July traditions have altered. We still go to a parade—it just happens to be in Bethany. Lisa and I are usually the only ones from the Haws family who will get up and make the trek to 39th Street Expressway. We love the Bethany parade. It has such a small-town feel to it. Afterward we make our way to Swadley's BBQ and eat lunch. Then it's time to watch the latest stage of the Tour de France. Between watching the bike race and snoozing on the couch, we wake up to prepare ourselves for the Nathan's Hot Dog Eating Championship.

The cofounder, George Shea, would declare the show to be the greatest event in sports. Mr. Shea goes over the top quite often. This is one of his typical introductions: "Yasir Salem [a contestant] is entirely committed to competitive eating. He will do whatever it takes to win. Three days ago he broke up with his girlfriend and euthanized his dog to leave a void of emptiness inside him that he could fill today with hot dogs and buns."

Professional eaters from across the country gather at Coney Island to consume as many hot dogs as they can in ten minutes. The current record is held by Joey Chestnut. In 2013 Chestnut ate sixty-nine hot dogs in the allotted ten-minute time period. The rules of the contest are pretty straightforward: Eat as many as you can in ten minutes without a "reversal." If you have a reversal of fortune, you're disqualified.

I've never been a big eater. In fact, I had a bad hot dog experience once at an Oklahoma drive-in and still have problems getting up the nerve to eat another dog. The only food-eating contest I might stand a chance winning is a Krispy Kreme donut duel. There's something about those warm donuts that triggers a genetic button deep within my bowels. I can eat a dozen in one walk past the box. My blood pressure is going up right now just thinking about it.

Then I remember the story about the World War II soldier on rest and relaxation in Paris. He had survived some horrific fighting and was due some time away from the front. He walked by a pastry shop and just had to have a donut. He ended up eating near thirty. Unfortunately, he developed botulism from the wad of undigested sugary dough in his stomach and died. I have to remind myself of the soldier story every time I see a box of Krispy Kremes.

Once I watch the hot dog eating contest, it becomes clear that we humans are a bunch of knuckleheads. I can only imagine God shaking His head at some of the strange things we do.

A good friend of mine sent me an audio recording of a sermon her sister had preached recently down in Georgetown,

Texas. Jennifer Bergland did a great job speaking God's word to an Oklahoma guy she doesn't even know. Sister Bergland referenced the story of Naomi, found in the book of Ruth. Through the story she reminded us that we serve a God of reversals. He can take a life season as sick-looking as one from a hot dog eating contest and make it beautiful. Our God can take what seems like an impossible situation and reverse it.

Take Naomi, for instance, one of the main characters from the story in Ruth. She and her husband, along with their two sons, were living in the midst of a famine and hurting for food. They decided to leave their country and move to a foreign land in search of a better life. Things got worse. Naomi's husband died. Then her sons married a couple of foreign women, which broke family tradition. Before long these men also died.

Naomi was left in a foreign land with her two foreign daughters-in-law and no security. She decided to go home, telling her two daughters-in-law to stay with their families. One of the ladies eventually did just that while the other, Ruth, said she wasn't leaving Noami's side. They made their way back home, but Naomi was really upset and even changed her name from Naomi (which means "pleasant") to Mara (which means "bitter").

Naomi was mad at God. She was disappointed with what life had thrown her way. She knew God could have prevented any of it, but He hadn't, and Naomi was bitter. What she didn't know was that the God she served hadn't abandoned her. He was at work. When Naomi and Ruth arrived back home, the people in town hardly recognized her. It had obviously been a rough ten years.

Naomi sent Ruth to a nearby field to try to gather some food for them to eat. In Ruth 2:3 we get our first sign that God is all over this situation: *So she went out, entered a field and began to glean behind the harvesters. As it turned out, she was working in a field belonging to Boaz, who was from the clan of Elimelek.* Did you see the code words? *As it turned out.* Have you had any of those moments—when God's plan was in action and you didn't even recognize it?

Many times it's only as we look back that we see God's intervention. When you're hungry, mad, depressed, and scared, it can be hard to see Him working. Praise the Lord—God doesn't wait for us to get our attitude all lined up before He acts. Ruth entered a field owned by Boaz, who was from the clan of Elimelek. Boaz was related to Naomi's former husband. Of all the fields she could have entered, she went to this particular field. And it just so happened (more code words) that the owner of the field, Boaz, was present. And wouldn't you know it? (code words)—Boaz and Ruth met. Before all is said and done, Boaz redeems Naomi's land for her, Ruth and Boaz fall in love, and they get married. Out of nowhere Naomi's situation is reversed. One moment Naomi has absolutely no future, and the next thing you know God has reversed it.

This is what I love about God. His plans are bigger than anything we could ever believe or hope to understand. When we put our trust in God, He can take a situation that appears hopeless, impossible, and unfixable and reverse it multiple times over. When God reversed Naomi's situation, He didn't just reverse her life's path. God works on a grander scale than that. Boaz and Ruth had a child named Obed, who became the father of Jesse. Jesse was the father of David. Yes, that was King David, whose entire family was from Bethlehem.

Several generations later—"There were shepherds living out in the fields nearby, keeping watch over their flocks at night. An angel of the Lord appeared to them, and the glory of the Lord shone around them, and they were terrified. But the angel said to them, 'Do not be afraid. I bring you good news that will cause great joy for all the people. Today in the town of David a Savior has been born to you; he is the Messiah, the Lord'" (Luke 2:8–11).

God not only reversed Naomi's and Ruth's life, but He reversed ours too! Through Naomi's situation we too were redeemed. We serve a God who likes to run the reverse. God also likes to use people like Boaz to help carry out the plan. Praying for someone? Maybe a kid from Bethany with a spinal cord injury? Feel led to take a neighbor some food? Ask a person to lunch so you can get to know him or her? Is God telling you to send a check somewhere? God loves to use His people to participate in the big reverse. Listen to Him. You just may be the pivotal person in His latest reversal.

God is in the midst of working a reverse out in our situation. I can see and feel it happening all around me. Thank you for being one of the people God is using in our lives.

Your prayers are important. Our story is not over yet! Thank you, Sister Bergland, for your great sermon! I am posting a link to it. If you get a chance you should listen to it! *http://gcnaz.org/media*

Do you not know? Have you not heard?
The Lord is the everlasting God, the Creator of the ends
of the earth. He will not grow tired or weary, and his under-
standing no one can fathom. He gives strength to the weary
and increases the power of the weak. Even youths grow tired
and weary, and young men stumble and fall; but those who
hope in the Lord will renew their strength. They will soar
on wings like eagles; they will run and not grow weary,
they will walk and not be faint
(Isaiah 40:28–31).

———— ┼ ┼ ————

The Grass is Always Greener

When I finally reached the age to hunt by myself, I could not contain my excitement. Having gone through the state of Oklahoma's hunter safety program and my dad's much more rigorous demands, I was allowed to carry my own 30-30 Winchester. Dad gave me five cartridges with strict instructions to always account for each and every shell. He dropped me off at my hunting spot and told me that he would pick me up just after dark.

I watched him make his way through the woods and out of sight. I scanned the forest for any sign of movement. It wasn't long before I observed a spot through the trees that appeared to be a little more advantageous for seeing deer, so I grabbed my gun and made my way to the "greener grass." Repositioning myself, I prepared for a massive buck to waltz toward me through the woods. After half an hour, I noticed another spot that looked like a "sure thing." I silently stalked my way to the new kill zone, sat down against a tree, and tried to blend in.

As the daylight began to fade, I decided to take a shortcut back to my original drop-off point. Moving as silently as possible, I hoped to get that last chance at a mossy-horned monster buck. I hadn't noticed that a storm was building and seemed to be moving in over the ridge. As I walked the path, it started sprinkling. Then the heavens opened up and the water was turned loose. I decided to head back to camp.

It wasn't long before I realized that I had no flashlight, rain gear, or idea of where I was going. Once-dry creek beds began rushing with water. Lightning filled the sky. My shoes began gathering sticky mud and weighing hundreds of pounds as I bulldozed through the underbrush. It's what search-and-rescue teams call a yard sale: I was dropping gear, wet gloves, and other outer garments as I searched for any sign of camp. I did cling to my rifle as a source of security in the growing panic.

Then I saw it—a campfire. By some miracle I had found my way back to camp. I was saved! As I walked nearer to the fire, I noticed that it was huge. I picked up my pace. As I approached I began to realize that I was wrong. This wasn't camp—apparently a bolt of lightning had struck a tree and set it ablaze. I warmed my hands near the tree and tried to regroup.-

Then an idea hit me: use the old shoot-your-gun-into-the-air trick. Fire three shots, and when the main camp returns fire I'll know how to get home. I stepped away from the tree, raised my rifle, and squeezed off three rounds. The gun roared with each shot. I listened intently for the return message, and my heart leapt when I heard the return shots. Then it sank as each echoed multiple times from all different directions. There was no way I was going to find my way back.

I decided on a new strategy. Surely one cannot walk in a straight line in Oklahoma forever before you find a road, so I picked my direction and marched. Eventually I did find a road and made it back to camp. As I sat by the fire to warm up, I destroyed a six-pack of orange Crush soda. I remember as if it were yesterday the look in my father's eyes when I did stumble back into camp. Our hunting party had gone out several times looking for me but were blocked by creeks that were overflowing their banks.

The panic and fear my dad must have felt when I was lost were things I could only imagine. I now know what deep panic and fear feel like when one of your kids is in a tough spot. I wish there were a shortcut in our current situation—it would be so great for all this to be over and to get back to normal. I have all sorts of scenarios that I believe would be great endings to Hudson's injury. Then I remember the chorus "I Have Decided to Follow Jesus." There's a reason we don't sing, "I have decided to show Jesus what to do." Many of us have tried that and we end up stumbling around in the dark, muddy and lost. I know in my heart that God is going to get us through this, but the journey isn't fun.

A friend of ours (thanks, M. A. K.!) sent a passage of Scripture that echoes where I am right now. I added a couple of verses to the beginning because I can relate to them as well. The passage is from Lamentations 3:18–25:

So I say, "My splendor is gone and all that I had hoped from the Lord." I remember my affliction and my wandering, the bitterness and the gall. I well remember them, and my soul is downcast within me. Yet this I call to mind and therefore I have hope: Because of the Lord's great love we are not consumed, for his compassions never fail. They are new every morning; great is your faithfulness. I say to myself, "The Lord is my portion; therefore I will wait for him." The Lord is good to those whose hope is in him, to the one who seeks him.

That is what we are going to do. We are going to hope. We are going to give thanks for God's great love, faithfulness, and compassion. We are going to give thanks for all the things He has done and is doing right now. We are going to seek Him and we are going to wait expectantly. We have decided to follow Jesus—no turning back, no turning back.

I called out to the Lord, out of my distress,
and He answered me; out of the belly of Sheol
I cried, and you heard my voice
(Jonah 2:2 ESV).

20

The Big Picture

I learned a lot of lessons from my dad. Had I paid better attention, I would have learned a lot more. In November 2003 I happened to be dialed in. I was taking dad on his last deer hunt. He had been battling cancer for a couple of years and we knew he was nearing the end. The cancer had spread to his brain and was wreaking havoc.

It was a gorgeous November day. Dad and I went to a farm we have permission to hunt on near Hydro, Oklahoma. I drove dad across the pasture and put him in a ground blind, telling him I would pick him up just after dark. After arriving at my hunting spot and settling in for the evening, I didn't hunt much at all but instead spent my time praying that my dad would get a chance to harvest a deer.

As the sun settled below the horizon, I was disappointed—I had not heard the sound of my dad's gun roaring through the chilled air. As I made my way back to the ground blind that held my dad, I noticed that he wasn't stepping out of the cover.

Parking the truck and getting out, I was met with silence. No sign of dad. I called his name. Nothing. It was at that point that I got the attention of nearly every wild animal in Blaine County. I began yelling my dad's name and searching the nearby creek. Nothing.

I decided to go to the landowner's house to get extra help and lights. As I pulled into their driveway, I could see through the kitchen window. Seated at the table was my dad and the landowner drinking coffee and talking casually. I did not enter the house in a very good mood. Very upset, I said, "Dad! What are you doing? I've been looking all over the place for you! How did you get here?" My dad just smiled at me and said he got too cold and called the landowner to come get him. They had been drinking coffee for the last hour. Uugghh!

On the way home I asked my dad if he had seen any deer.

He replied, "No, but did you see that amazing sunset?" He went on and on about it, describing the vivid colors that had lit up the sky. Once again my earthly father reminded me that God's creation holds countless blessings. I wonder how many times I've missed a blessing because I was too focused on what I felt was important and not on what God was putting right in front of me.

As I sat in Hudson's team meeting recently I heard that still quiet voice ask, *Are you too focused on Hudson's miracle to see other opportunities I've placed right in front of you?* As I think about our doctors, therapists, and the host of nurses and techs, I pray that I hear and obey the Spirit's direction. I trust that God is going to take care of Hudson. I hope He can trust me to keep my head up along the way so that I don't miss the big picture.

You answer us with awesome and righteous deeds,
God our Savior, the hope of all the ends of the earth and
of the farthest seas, who formed the mountains by your power,
having armed yourself with strength, who stilled the roaring
of the seas, the roaring of their waves, and the turmoil of the
nations. The whole earth is filled with awe at
your wonders; where morning dawns, where evening
fades, you call forth songs of joy
(Psalm 65:5–8).

Snowball

It's been a couple of weeks since it snowed here in Denver. That has now changed. It looks as if three different snowstorms will hit in less than seven days. Hudson has been through the grinder again today. The day started off with another round of manual therapy. This is where they stick needles into tight muscles and then manually move them around. I think there is a sign in the office that says "No Pain, No Gain."

Hudson showed improvement in every area during weight lifting today. He got another round of electric therapy that targeted his triceps. We also practiced transferring him into a regular car. If we can get that down, then we can haul him out of this place and do some excursions. That would be awesome! In the meantime, we keep at it one day at a time. Right now we'll hunker down since we're under a winter weather advisory. It won't be the first time I've been hit by snow.

My first horse was named Snowball. We inherited him from some "friends." A more appropriate name for this horse would have been "Lucifer." From the very beginning Snowball and I had a love-hate relationship. He loved to hate me. I remember the first time I rode him. After a two-hour bribing session holding out a carrot in front of me with a rope behind my back, I was finally able to catch him and saddle him up. At this time I had no idea that Snowball was one of the horses straight out of Revelation.

Our ride out across the pasture was just as I imagined. I was the Lone Ranger riding Silver. Then we made the turn for home and off we went. Little to my knowledge, Snowball had pulled the old trick of bloating his stomach while I tried to cinch down the saddle. I enjoyed the first ten yards, but as the loud snorting and strings of snot started pouring back on me, I decided to shut him down and pulled back on the reins. We gained speed. I pulled harder. We hit warp speed 7. As I stood in the stirrups and pulled with all my might, I felt the first slip of the saddle. As we neared warp 9 the saddle slid completely sideways. As only a kid could think, I was trying to figure out just how bad it was going to hurt when the saddle and I went completely under Snowball. I didn't have time to find out. The saddle came loose and we went flying, Snowball racing across the pasture laughing like a hyena and I falling into the middle of the biggest sticker patch in Pittsburgh County. I remember that we stopped counting stickers when we hit one hundred twenty-five.

For some reason we kept that horse and continued trying to ride him. If you could catch him, you had to prepare for a variety of pain-inflicting tactics that Snowball had planned for you. His favorites were to run you under every low-hanging branch on the farm. After that, he would run you along the barbed wire fence. Still in the saddle? Then you got to experience an actual horse bite. Fun times.

I'll never forget the day my cousin came over and wanted to ride a horse. Dad reminded us that we hadn't ridden Snowball recently and it was time to give him a workout. After our three-hour bribe-and-chase session, we got Snowball saddled. I said a kid version of last rites to my cousin and hoisted him into the saddle and dove for cover.

What Snowball didn't know is that my cousin is the toughest human I know. I watched in amazement as Snowball began his procession of pain. He ran under every tree. My cousin stayed on though his shirt was ripped and he was bleeding from tree limb scratches. Then came the barbed wire. Cousin 2, Snowball 0. Then Snowball turned into Cujo and tried biting my cousin's legs. Nothing but a mouth full of jeans. Then Snowball lost it. He began bucking wildly. I couldn't tell if the guttural noises I was hearing were from Snowball or my cousin. Yet to my amazement, my cousin was still mounted. He looked as if he were right out of the National Finals Rodeo. As Snowball tired, I expected him just to give up and trot around the pasture. *Nada.* With a final burst of strength, Snowball reared back and did a back-buster right on top of my cousin. It wasn't a normal back buster—it was one of those jump-way-up-in-the-air, land, twist-it-into-the-ground-and-just-lie-there backbusters. I froze. I didn't know what to do. Snowball leapt to his feet, made a mad dash, jumped over a five-strand barbed wire fence, and took off down the county road. My cousin limped up to the house, bruised but not broken.

A few days later a man knocked on our door and asked us if we were missing a horse. My dad looked him in the eye and said, "Nope—all our horses are accounted for." I saw Snowball a couple of times over the years in a pasture down the road. I even saw someone chasing him with some food and a rope. I've thought of that horse many times over the years.

There are some days that I feel as if I've gone a couple of rounds with Snowball. I feel bruised, scratched, and trying to dust myself off. Some days I wonder if I'm more like him than I would like to admit. When God has tried to provide some guidance and direction, to reign me in, have I accepted it? I wonder how many blessings I've missed out on because I was so worried about stuff. Have I been focused on what I want to do and missed out on just spending some time with Him? Time with Jesus is what I crave these days—more of Him and His guidance. And despite all those times over the years when I ran, fought, and turned my back on Him, His response is "Welcome back! I've been looking all over for you!"

Blessed is the one who trusts in the Lord, whose confidence is in him. They will be like a tree planted by the water that sends out its roots by the stream. It does not fear when heat comes; its leaves are always green. It has no worries in a year of drought and never fails to bear fruit (Jeremiah 17:7–8).

The Trail 70

During my growing-up years, our family were the proud owners of a Honda Trail 70 motorcycle. We had several other larger dirt bikes but could seldom get them to run. The Honda would typically start after sixty or seventy attempts, so it was our go-to transportation around the homestead. To say we put that bike through its paces is a severe understatement.

One must remember that these were the days of Evel Knievel. We jumped that bike over flower gardens, ditches, cars, and people. We chased armed felons across the countryside as we imagined we were Ponch or John from the *ChiPs* television show. Because of the big tires, it also served as a ski lift. We would sled down our long driveway, across the county road through the open gate of our neighbor's pasture, and then catch a ride on the Honda back to the top.

That Honda also served as my racing bike on the Haws International Raceway, which was mapped out in the lower pasture. As the proud owner of the course record, I was always trying to set a personal record. One Sunday after church a friend of mine spent the afternoon at our house. To my horror, he broke my course record. It was on. I had made a couple of attempts to regain my title when I heard my dad's whistle, which meant "Get your bootie to the house right now!" I had to try one more time. As I was making my way through turn three, I struck one of the many rocks on the course, which threw my bike into a wicked dance of death. I decided to bail during one of the dips. Unfortunately, the bike bounced back toward me.

Before the dust had even cleared, I knew I was in trouble. The bike ended up on top of me with the engine lying on my left leg. In my haste to get on the bike that day, I had slipped on a pair of shorts. By the time my friend had pulled the bike off me, I knew it was *no bueno*. Worse yet, I knew I was going to be in trouble with my dad because we had a standing rule against wearing shorts while riding motorcycles.

Remembering the earlier whistle, we made our way back to the house. In order to hide the evidence, I pulled my church socks up over the gnarled flesh. I made it about halfway through supper before I couldn't take it anymore. I had to come clean. That little episode left a second-degree burn from my knee to my ankle. I got numerous reminders over the next several months about the no-shorts rule. Despite my best attempts, some article of clothing would adhere to that wound and we would have to free the skin using a combination of screaming and peeling. I would sing Johnny Cash's "Ring of Fire" at the top of my voice.

I'm sorry to say that wasn't the first or the last time I've tried to hide my poor choices. I guess we humans have been doing stuff like that from the beginning of our existence. When I read the genealogy of Jesus I can see some folks who fit into the poor choice category. Rahab, a prostitute, is there. King David was guilty of adultery and murder. Abraham claimed his wife was his sister and let a local ruler take her into his harem— in fact, he did that twice. Yet here they are in the lineage of Jesus. I think God is sending us a very clear message: "I know you're not perfect. I know you make mistakes. Don't pull up your socks and try to cover up your flaws. Give them to Me. I'm a lot like a Honda Trail 70. I can do anything."

Jesus did many other things as well. If every one of them were written down, I suppose that even the whole world would not have room for the books that would be written (John 21:25).

23

Restoration

My dad loved working on old cars. At any given time we would have at least twelve "projects" parked back behind our house. If it weren't for the trees blocking the view, most people would have thought our homestead was a salvage yard. My dad was always on the lookout for his next diamond in the rough.

We would be driving down the road and all of a sudden be whipping a U-turn. My dad had eagle vision when it came to spotting wild game, hidden fishing holes, and classic cars. Got a 1940 Ford parked under a tarp behind the barn in head high weeds? Didn't matter. My dad could spot it going 65 mph past your place at night. What this meant to a kid was an hour waiting in the car while he looked it over and haggled with the owner over a price. Then we would have to make a return trip with a trailer or towrope.

I've tried to steer more disabled cars down the road while being pulled by my dad's truck than I care to remember. Some of the projects took longer than others. Some were completely miraculous. What started out as a pile of rust was transformed into a head-turner. Each of these former rust buckets was turned into a ride that caused people to stop and stare, asking, "What year is that model?"

I'll never forget the day my siblings and I got off the school bus and were running home to watch *Star Trek*. Two fire trucks were coming down our driveway. We raced to the house to discover that some embers from our trash barrels had escaped and caught the pasture on fire. By the time the fire department had arrived, four of my dad's "babies" had burned up.

When my dad got home from work, it was after dark. Because I was the source of most catastrophes around my house, I quickly informed my father that I had nothing to do with his loss. In other words, I threw my mom under the bus. My dad was outside for a long time that night. I don't know what he did out there. It was one of those moments as a kid when you know it's best to be out of sight and out of mind.

One of the vehicles that was toasted was a Studebaker pickup truck. I think it was one of the cars that actually blew up. Despite its mangled appearance after the fire, my dad still had a vision for it. He cut the bed off of the cab and turned it into a cool-looking trailer, painting it lime green in honor of the 1970s. That trailer was put to use for many years.

I know another Father who is in the restoration business, who searches high and low for lost diamonds in the rough—someone who looks beyond the rust or charred remains and sees new creations, taking broken lives, situations, and bodies and transforming them into head-turners.

Not only is God restoring Hudson, but I wanted to update you on some of His other projects. Caleb, the young man we met at the OU Medical Center with the traumatic brain injury (who doctors said would need to go to long-term care) is walking and talking. His short-term memory is improving daily. Hayden, the young man we met here at Craig Hospital who had suffered a serious brain injury (the doctors said he wasn't going to make it when they wheeled him into the trauma unit the day of his accident as his eyes were fixed and dilated), got to go home today. He walked out today with his mom and grandma (who is from Oklahoma). His last words to me were "I'll be praying for Hudson." God is good!

The God of all grace, who called you to his
eternal glory in Christ, after you have suffered a little
while, will himself restore you and make you strong,
firm and steadfast. To him be the
power for ever and ever. Amen
(1 Peter 5:10–11).

24

Swing Away

Hudson, Lisa, and I are at our apartment in the Denver area. Craig Hospital provides family housing. It is an efficiency apartment and a huge blessing. We are five minutes from our door to Hudson's room—probably two minutes if I were in shape and hit the stairs. They worked him over pretty good today during physical therapy. Hudson is making progress daily. They are baby steps, but we'll take it. For instance, he is showing better control of his upper body. He still doesn't have feeling from the chest down, but we're working those muscles regardless.

Another area we could use prayer for is hydration. He isn't drinking enough water. His appetite is coming back slowly but we really need him to drastically increase his fluids.

Hudson had his urology evaluation this morning. I've never wished physical pain on my kids before, but I did today. I was hoping what is a painful procedure would register on Hudson's radar. It didn't register but at least they were able to clean some stuff out of his bladder.

I have been thinking about the subject of pain. Believe it or not, it reminded me of something that happened to me when I was around ten years old and played baseball for the Edmond (Oklahoma) Eagles. I was not the biggest kid in the world and used that to my advantage when I learned about this thing called the "strike zone." I would shrink my 4'1" frame as compactly as possible to draw a walk—just squat down on each pitch, and four pitches later I was off to first base. This tactic served me well for several seasons. Why did I use this strategy? I was scared of the ball. It's easier to dodge a baseball if you don't have to worry about swinging the bat.

My baseball career took a turn in a game against the Hawks, the best team in the ten-year-old league, as we faced their hardest-throwing pitcher. I was implementing my normal strategy of squat-and-watch when for some insane reason I decided to actually swing. As I did so, the inside pitch struck my hands and fouled off to the screen. I went down as if a sniper had picked me off.

I flopped around like a fish out of water and cried like a baby. I was sure I had compound fractures of both hands! After composing myself, I jumped up and jogged to first base. That's when I hear, "Son, come back here—that was a foul ball!" to which I replied, "Mr. Umpire, that hit me and I get first base!" I then learned about this crazy rule in baseball where your hands are supposedly part of the bat.

As I reentered the batter's box, I was angry. A tremendous injustice was being done to a ten-year-old. Baseball 101: Hit by pitch, get a free base. That's American baseball. Apparently we were now playing communist baseball. I squeezed the bat hard and eyed the pitcher through mad and watery eyes. As the fastball approached, my second act of insanity occurred that day: I swung again. This time I connected. The ball sailed to the fence and I had a stand-up double. I was never again afraid of the ball from that day forward.

Without the pain and agony of that day, I would have never experienced the full joy of playing the game of baseball. Baseball, like life, is a participation sport. Sure, I struck out many times after that pivotal day, but it sure feels better going down swinging.

I'm now going through another kind of pain and agony. Watching my son battle a serious injury is far worse pain than any other I've ever experienced or imagined. It fits into that category of things parents fear the most for their children.

God has reminded me, however, that pain and suffering don't have to have the last word. If we allow Him to pour more of Himself into us, we can emerge victorious. When we rely on Him for courage to get back in there, He is faithful. I have no doubt that our family will enjoy and appreciate life to a much deeper level. That is already happening. Right now we're getting up, dusting ourselves off, and stepping back into the box. The only difference between that game way back when and Hudson's situation today is that I'm not looking for a double—I'm looking for a home run.

So do not fear, for I am with you;
do not be dismayed, for I am your God.
I will strengthen you and help you;
I will uphold you with my righteous right hand
(Isaiah 41:10).

Let's Rodeo

During my sophomore year in high school, I served as a teacher's aide for my baseball coach first thing in the morning. I would grade papers, run copies, get him coffee, and so on. It was a blow-off hour for me. Those were the days!

Like most sixteen-year-olds, I began taking advantage of my position. I would leisurely stroll around campus before school started, knowing that I didn't have a "real" first hour. One day after making my late appearance for the forty-second time, my coach issued a decree. "Haws", he said, "if you're late one more time, you and I are going to go rodeo."

If you went to Edmond Mid-High School in 1980, you knew what the phrase "go rodeo" meant. It had nothing to do with cowboys or livestock. The teacher next to my coach's room had a paddle mounted above his chalkboard. On that paddle was a bumper sticker with the Marlboro man on it and the words "Let's Go Rodeo." My coach's ultimatum got my attention. Being that he was a baseball coach, I knew he could swing the lumber. I made a mental note right then and there to be early the next day.

When the next day showed up, my "get there early" plan was in full implementation. The plan hit a big snag when I got into my truck and the battery was dead. I hit the panic button and began racing around my dad's junky shed looking for jumper cables. No luck. I decided to take the Walton truck to school. Since it had a top speed of 28 mph going downhill with the clutch pushed in, I didn't make very good time. I would like to say that I screeched and squealed the tires as I made my way into the school parking lot, but the Walton truck had never squealed a tire in its life.

I bailed out of the vehicle and sprinted into the school. Coach's room was on the second floor at the far end of the hall. I took the steps three at a time. The halls were clear and I knew the tardy bell was fixing to ring. I could see my coach and the guy who taught next to him standing outside the doors of their classrooms as I ran down the hall as fast as I could.

The bell rang when I was within ten feet of the door, and I ran through the doorway leaning forward like an Olympian through the finish line. I could still hear the echo of the tardy bell and for a second thought I had made it. I turned to see my coach sticking his head in the doorway and saying, "Haws, you're late. It's rodeo time." The whole class looked at me with wide, fearful eyes. I even heard someone declare that I was a dead man. I turned and walked out into the hall.

Coach told me to go get the paddle. Now for a second time a whole classroom of kids stared at me like a convicted killer. I walked over and lifted the paddle from its home. It felt surprisingly heavy with its thick leather wrist strap laced through a hole in the handle. The multiple layers of shellac reflected the classroom lights.

I reentered the hallway with the implement of death and awaited instructions. The two teachers talked casually. The owner of the paddle was a huge guy, one of the first bodybuilders I had ever seen in person. He had guns on him that at that particular moment rivaled Arnold Swartzenegger's. They left me on ice for a while; then Coach turned his attention to me. "Haws, did I not just yesterday tell you not to be late?" I acknowledged the fact and began explaining my sad little tale. He listened to the whole story and then explained that had I been on time consistently, I wouldn't be about to ride the lightning for this tardy. Thus the ritual began.

I knew the drill well. I was asked to empty my pockets and was then directed to brace myself on the wall atop the stairwell. I could see him loosening up as if he were about to go a few rounds with Ali. I was like "Holy smokes—this guy is going to let her rip." And let her rip he did. He was smooth about it, though. Despite being told to keep my eyes forward, I was trying to catch a glimpse out of my peripheral vision in order to trigger my gluteus maximus muscles to lock down as tight as possible. He would act as if he were pulling the trigger and then stop at the last second. When the trigger was pulled, it sounded like a forty caliber went off. Then my glutes sent my brain a message: they were on fire.

I buckled against the wall. It was everything I could do to keep my composure. I could hear kids saying ooos and aah's from the rooms nearby. I had been correct in my assessment regarding my coach's ability to swing a stick. He quickly jumped to number one on the list of the all-time worst persons you wanted giving you swats.

What happened next was crazy. He told me to get ready—I was getting another one. My head jerked around so fast I almost passed out. My brain went into panic mode. It was everything I could do to keep my composure after one swat. I was going to be destroyed if I had to go for another ride. I began to beg and plead. Was there any other way? Could I wash his car? Pay him money? Anything? He looked at me for what seemed like an eternity. He then declared a deal. If I did a hundred push-ups without stopping, we were good. If I stopped short for any reason, we would rodeo again.

So on that day I did one hundred perfect push-ups without stopping. He kept his word, and in return I was never late again. Some of you might think my coach a harsh man. He wasn't. I loved him. He shaped my life in many ways. He taught me how to play the game of baseball at a higher level. He taught me to push myself to levels I didn't think possible. I deserved the punishment I received that morning. In fact, I deserved to go a second round. He showed me mercy.

I think about mercy a lot, especially as we near Easter. I wish I could say that my worst transgression against God was being late. It is not. I'm not alone this time. We have all sinned and fallen short. Sometimes our reaction to this fact is to try to be good enough to please God. The world is full of religious practices designed to earn one's way to heaven. They too fall short. We are all guilty and don't deserve anything good from God.

So what does He do? When we can't make it to Him, He comes to us. We have a Savior. When we receive Jesus and His gift of grace, our sins are no more. They are blotted out. Our scarlet sin is made whiter than snow. The slate is cleaned. Our sin is removed from us as far as the east is from the west. God put the wrong on Him who never did anything wrong so we could be put right with God. We deserve the stairwell wall—we get grace. Amazing.

God so loved the world that he gave his
one and only Son, that whoever believes in him shall
not perish but have eternal life. For God did not send his
Son into the world to condemn the world,
but to save the world through him
(John 3:16–17).

26

Promises

Lisa and I attended a wedding last night. Every time I go to a wedding it causes me to reflect back on August 16, 1986, my own wedding day. Thankfully Lisa and I were married at 10 am because it turned out to be a really hot day.

Lisa is a perfect match for me. We have our common strengths. We have strengths we uniquely possess that accentuate each other.

I remember like yesterday our first date. I was waiting in the lobby of her college dorm when she emerged out of the stairwell. I felt like a high school baseball player who was just about to face a major league pitcher. She was way out of my league.

A little over three years later we were honeymooning in Eureka Springs, Arkansas. We borrowed my in-laws' car for the trip. When it was time for refueling, I couldn't open the gas flap on the car. The car was a newer model and I didn't feel it would be proper for me to rip the cover off the fuel tank. After fifteen to twenty minutes of futile effort, we had to call Lisa's dad on a pay phone to ask him how to get to the fuel tank. We had just enough change to make a thirty-second call. We filled the coin slot with nickels, dimes, and quarters, and Lisa was able to get the problem communicated and the solution from her dad before we were cut off. Turns out the car had this brand-new feature where you had to engage a lever to open the fuel lid. I bet Lisa's dad was wondering just who in the world he had given his daughter away to earlier that day—the guy couldn't even put gas in the car!

As I watched the bride and groom make promises to each other last night, I was reminded of the promises Lisa and I made to each other almost thirty years ago—to love and care for each other for the rest of our lives. When things were going great and when things were not going as planned, to love each other if we were blessed with resources or if we struggled from check to check—we promised to love each other during healthy times and when illness or injury showed up. We promised to seek God's counsel and to raise our future children in the church. We promised before God, just as the two young people did last night, that we would keep these promises for the rest of our lives.

As I drove home after the awesome reception, I was thinking about the promises we make to God. I have made several new ones the past four months. I wish I would have written down all the promises I've made to God. I fear there are some

I may have forgotten over the years. We humans tend to do stuff like that.

We serve a God who also makes promises. His promises are written down. He isn't afraid for us to hold Him accountable. He hasn't boasted or claimed anything He isn't willing to do. We are His and He wants us to know what it means to be children of God. For instance, He tells us we can do all things through Him. He will give us strength. He promises us rest. There is nothing in all of creation that will separate us from His love. He hears our prayers. He sees our tears. He has a plan for our future and it is filled with hope. He is slow to anger and full of compassionate love. He knows each of us and has designed us uniquely for His purposes. We are uniquely and wonderfully made. He promises that He will keep us in the palm of His hand and that no one can snatch us from it.

He promises us that His word is true. He says He carries our burdens every day. He looks after the sparrows; certainly He will look after us as well. He is our Shepherd; we shall not want for anything. When we call on Him, when we come and pray to Him, He promises that He will listen. When we seek Him, He promises that we will find Him. He promises to be our shield, our glory, and the lifter of our heads when we're down. He promises to build us up. He promises not to change like shifting shadows. His unfailing love toward us will not be shaken. He promises that the good things He has planned for us are too numerous to count. He promises to make our deserts like Eden, our wastelands like gardens. He promises us power when we are weak. He promises to rescue us when we are in trouble. He promises to make ways for us when we can't find our way. He promises never to leave us. He promises that if we will ask anything in the name of Jesus, He will do it.

To show us He means what He says, He sent His Son into the world to die for us. Jesus is God's promises in action. He took our sin with Him to a cross. He suffered for us so we could spend eternity with Him.

I'm going to keep the promises I made to Lisa until the day I die. Every time I go to a wedding, I pray the couple's marriage will be as wonderful as ours has been. I pray that they will keep their promises. Over the last thirty years (and especially the past four months) God has kept His promises to the Haws family. He is faithful. He is wonderful. He is our hope.

God is not human, that he should lie,
not a human being, that he should change his mind.
Does he speak and then not act? Does he promise and not fulfill?
(Numbers 23:19).

Through these he has given us his very great and
precious promises, so that through them you may participate
in the divine nature, having escaped the corruption in
the world caused by evil desires
(2 Peter 1:4).

27

Heisman Talk

A reporter from a national magazine called me several weeks ago. She said they were doing a story about football and wanted to ask me some questions about Hudson's injury. It seemed from the line of questioning that the writer was wanting me to say something about the dangers of the game. She asked me if I resented football.

My dad introduced football to me. He was a standout high school football player and two-time state champion wrestler. The University of Oklahoma awarded him a double scholarship, and Dad became a Sooner in 1958. After his freshman year he was called to Coach Bud Wilkinson's office. Dad told me that he was very nervous waiting to see the football coach, running his last few days through his head trying to figure out if he had done something wrong.

Apparently, according to Coach Wilkinson, the wrestling coach believed my father had a great chance to be a national champion wrestler and didn't want to share him with football. My dad loved football but felt that the writing was on the wall.

However, during off-season wrestling practice in the old field house, Dad kept hearing something banging up against the window. Curiosity finally got the best of him. When he looked out the window, he saw the kicker practicing field goals, ball after ball bouncing off the field house.

My dad took it as a sign that he was to focus on football. He withdrew from OU and transferred to Central State University (now the University of Central Oklahoma). He then played guard on the offensive line and linebacker on defense. In 1962, my dad's senior year, Central State went undefeated and won the NAIA national championship.

My dad wrote me the letter you see on the next page when I was ten years old. You might think the ball didn't mean much to Dad. Why would he let two little boys mess with it? I believe it was because my dad loved the game and that it was his desire to foster that same love in his sons.

But isn't football dangerous? Why would a dad expose his son to something that could harm him? While at Craig Hospital we were surrounded by other patients who had been injured. Car wrecks, motorcycle accidents, blow-up bouncy house mishaps, body surfing accidents, tragic dives into the ocean—unless you live in a bubble, life can be dangerous.

My desire has always been for my boys to live a life of adventure. I don't think God designed a body that can run, jump, dive, swim, and roll just to hang out on the sidelines of life.

Solutions in
Viaflex
Plastic Containers

Jimmy,

Here is your football.
This ball is 12 years old. It
was the game ball during my
senior year at Central State.
The same year our team went
undefeated and won the National
Small College Championship. This
ball was used when we played
Northwestern Univ. at Alva Okla.
Use it to learn how to pass,
punt, and kick. If you remember
to put it up and not leave it
out in the rain, it will last
you another 12 years.

Love
Dad,

When you decide to get into the game, you have the chance to enjoy some of the best life has to offer. You get to take the path of discovery.

Football and life dispense lessons. You learn you can take more than you thought, how to trust your teammates, about being reliable and doing your job, giving maximum effort each and every play. You learn to reach goals and hopefully experience the joy of success. Along the way you will also face danger, adversity, and pain. Football and life are full of physical and emotional struggles.

In February 2016 we were honored to have four men who have been recognized as being part of an elite group of football players participate in a fundraiser for Hudson. I had an opportunity to say a few words to these childhood heroes:

> For a long time I assumed the Heisman Trophy was awarded to the best college football player of that particular year. But athletic ability is only part of it. The Heisman Memorial Trophy annually recognizes the outstanding college football player whose performance best exhibits the pursuit of excellence with integrity.
>
> Sam Bradford, I still cheer you on every time I see you play. You converted me to a Rams fan (which I no longer cheer for) and now an Eagles fan. I will cheer for the Eagles until the day you leave, because I am a Sam Bradford fan. Your helicopter move against

OSU will forever be burned in my memory. I have greatly admired your talent on the football field, but my best memory was at a golf tournament. Chris Chamberlain had hit a great shot within ten feet of the hole. I could hear him giving you some chin music. You stepped up and hit it within a foot, shutting up the trash talking. Impressive.

Jason White, I remember the roar of the crowd when the man on the PA announced that you had won the Heisman. We were at Owen Field winning Bethany High School's first football state championship. We were so proud of you! You showed a loyalty and work ethic that spoke volumes to me. I loved watching you throw the long ball. When I drive through Tuttle, I think of you and how you have represented Oklahoma well!

Billy Sims, as a kid you were the player I modeled my game after. Your high-knee stride and bulldozer mentality awed me as a young football player. I used to zigzag through my house, make believing I was you. It usually always ended with me jumping as high as I could over the unseen pile of defenders, landing in my bed, which served as the end zone. I was mesmerized by the passion in which you played the game.

Steve Owens, I never got to see you play in person. I was five years old when you won your Heisman. But I felt as if I had seen every game because my dad compared all running backs to you. You set a standard of toughness that carries on to this day. I went back and watched some game film of your OU days. If it weren't for your number, I would have insisted you were a middle linebacker running the ball. I'm glad I didn't have to tackle you.

As Heisman winners, you have been at the pinnacle. Your greatest athletic glory played out in front of millions. You made a difficult game look easy.

You have also faced tremendous adversity, devastating injuries that dished out tremendous amounts of pain and suffering. Much of the suffering was done well outside the public eye. You have felt the weight of doubt, slipping hope, and fear.

It is the competitive spirit that football develops that helps us get back up and fight. My dad wanted that for me and I wanted that for my sons. If I focused on only one play in October 2015 and forgot the countless others, I imagine resentment would be hard to fight off. But I do remember the countless other plays—the wonderful life lessons that my sons got to experience.

I asked Hudson before his senior year why he played football. Did he love the game? No. He loved the guys he played the game with. He loved the competitive struggle with his other brothers. Hudson has never been the biggest, fastest, or strongest. The other team wasn't eyeballing him in pregame warm-ups. But when the whistle blew, it wasn't long before you knew that 34 was a player. Hudson played with a tenacity that boggled the mind. He played like a warrior. I imagine he played a lot like my dad.

When Hudson was injured on October 23, 2015, another event happened that no one wrote about in the newspapers or reported in TV segments. It didn't show up in the box score. Yet two teams, two groups of young men, lined back up after one of their brothers was airlifted to the hospital. They strapped on their helmets and finished what was started—through tears, fear, doubt, and pain. They put on a display of courage most kids would never dream of accomplishing.

I remember that after Hudson woke up from surgery he couldn't talk because of the vent tube down his throat. But his question was clear. Who won? I wanted to lie and tell him Bethany, but I couldn't. Actually my heart told me two groups of young men had won that night.

Do I resent the game? No, I still have a love and respect for football. I'm thankful for the blessings it has help provide my family.

I'm thankful for my dad introducing me to football. However, you wouldn't be getting the whole story unless I told you about my mom. You see, my dad introduced me to football but my mom introduced me to Jesus. It was my mom who took us to church to expose us to a Savior who loves us beyond measure.

While football can be rewarding, bring you great fame, and teach you many lessons, my mom knew I needed a Savior. Football requires human effort, but our souls cry out for a divine touch. When your knee is blown out and cannot be repaired, when your dreams are crushed, when you have lost a loved one or he or she lies sick or injured and there's nothing you can do to fix it, when the weight of the world is on your shoulders and you have a pain so deep you can't breathe, you have a good Father who can heal the brokenhearted, set the captive free, make the lame to walk again, cause the blind to see. We have a Savior.

In order to have a divine relationship with Jesus, we have to surrender—something they don't teach us in football. Surrender to Christ sounds easy before you do it but seems so vague and unreal until you do.

All we have to do is say yes, and the relationship is set up. Jesus has already said His yes. All His barriers are down. When we say our yes to Jesus, we discover He is who He says He is.

He gives us rest when we are weary; He gives power to the weak and strength to the powerless; He does not leave us or forsake us; He takes care of us. He promises and delivers peace of mind that surpasses all human understanding. He seeks for us when we are lost. He gives us a future and a hope. He restores souls. His way is the Way. He is the Truth. He is the Life. He is the lover of our souls, our advocate, our friend.

Football will serve Hudson well as he continues rehabilitation. His strong work ethic and coaching ability will aid him. Doctors will do what they are able to do. But I know a man . . .

One day Jesus went across a lake. A large crowd had gathered.

> *Then one of the synagogue leaders, named Jairus, came, and when he saw Jesus, he fell at His feet. He pleaded earnestly with him* [I've done a whole lot of that myself], *"My little daughter is dying. Please come and put your hands on her so that she will be healed and live." So Jesus went with him. A large crowd followed and pressed around him. . . .*
>
> *While Jesus was still speaking, some people came from the house of Jairus, the synagogue leader. "Your daughter is dead," they said. "Why bother the teacher anymore?" Overhearing what they said, Jesus told him, "Don't be afraid; just believe." He did not let anyone follow him except Peter, James and John the brother*

of James. When they came to the home of the synagogue leader, Jesus saw a commotion, with people crying and wailing loudly. He went in and said to them, "Why all this commotion and wailing? The child is not dead but asleep." But they laughed at him.

After he put them all out, he took the child's father and mother and the disciples who were with him, and went in where the child was. He took her by the hand and said to her, "Talitha koum!" (which means "Little girl, I say to you, get up!"). Immediately the girl stood up and began to walk around (she was twelve years old). At this they were completely astonished. He gave strict orders not to let anyone know about this, and told them to give her something to eat.
(Mark 5:22–24, 35–43)

Ever since October 23 Jesus' message to me has been clear: *I have you! Trust Me! Do not be afraid—just believe.*

Do you not know? Have you not heard? The Lord is the everlasting God, the Creator of the ends of the earth. He will not grow tired or weary, and his understanding no one can fathom. He gives strength to the weary and increases the power of the weak. Even youths grow tired and weary, and young men stumble and fall; but those who hope in the Lord will renew their strength. They will soar on wings like eagles; they will run and not grow weary, they will walk and not be faint. (Isaiah 40:28–31)

I want to thank everyone again for their support. I thank Bobby Boyd, the quarterback/kicker for the 1958 Sooners who convinced my dad to transfer. I thank all of you for your continued prayers. The best part of Hudson's story is yet to be told. You're all invited to the celebration. It's going to be a good one!

28

Epilogue

As I write this epilogue, 2020 has arrived. Lisa and I spent New Year's Eve at home watching a movie and eating take out. Hudson is out with friends. There are several constants for us since October 23, 2015. The faithfulness of Hudson's friends has been one of those constants. Hudson is in his final semester of college. I have not had to take him to class one time. Each morning one of his buddies will show up and haul him off to campus. It is not convenient for them. The media hasn't descended to report of their efforts nor have they earned any earthly award. Yet here are these young men taking time out of their schedules to help out their friend. They have worked behind the scenes, out of the spotlight, day in and day out.

Another constant has been the lack of change in Hudson's injury. He continues to experience paralysis from mid-chest down. Hudson has no sensation below his injury line. He requires assistance in order to get up and at 'em for the day. Our battle with urinary tract infections, muscle spasms, and maintaining skin health keep us on our toes. We celebrated 2019 without a night's stay in the hospital. Amazing!

As we remain in the waiting, another constant has been the call from some pretty dark places. These exit ramps along our life's journey echo with the siren calls of doubt. While the exact wording may vary, the theme is from days of old: "Did God really say…?" Did He really say He would never leave you or forsake you? Did He really say He would give you a future and a hope? Did He really promise to supply every one of our needs: strength, peace, patience, hope, and trust?

I don't know where you are in your life's journey. Maybe things are incredible. You wake every morning without a care in the world. I imagine most of you are in the other group. Life has been messy, confusing, and has punched you in the gut a few times. I would be lying if I claimed the last four-plus years haven't had their challenges. Despite those challenges, I can still testify to the faithfulness of God.

God has faithfully sent the right people with the right words at just the right time. One example of this is represented in the picture you see on the next page. Each week for the last four-plus years a lady from Avo, Missouri, named Kathy has sent us a postcard. Written on each card is a verse containing one of God's promises. Each week we have received a reminder from a woman we have never met that God has not abandoned us.

God has provided a way when we couldn't see a way. We have risen every time we have been knocked down. We have hope. I don't know what today holds for you. My prayer is that you will cling to God. Draw near to Him; He has drawn near to you. If you are waiting for something to happen, hang on! Today just might be that day!

29

Photo Gallery

Hudson's senior picture. He played the bass violin in his school orchestra during middle and high school. Hudson was probably the only middle linebacker who also played the bass!

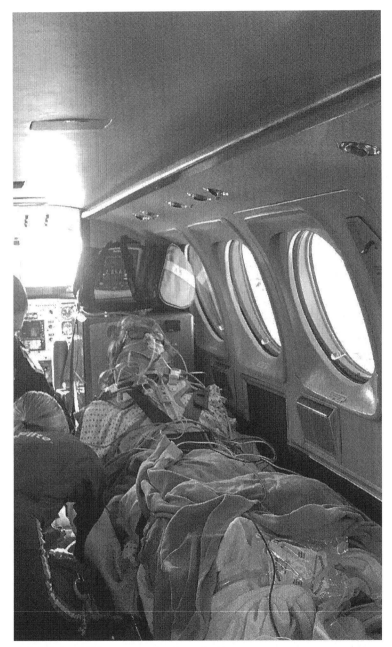

Medi-flight from Oklahoma City to Craig Hospital in Denver

Hudson's eighteenth birthday, just weeks after returning home from rehab

Hudson's first successful deer hunt post-injury

Hudson fishing at Roaring River State Park in Missouri

Hudson with his football brothers along with the University of Oklahoma's first four Heisman Trophy winners

Haws family

Hudson and crew exploring the Rocky Mountains during an annual re-evaluation trip to Colorado

Made in the USA
Coppell, TX
15 April 2022

76651778R00085